Modern Critical Interpretations

Ernest Hemingway's
The Sun Also Rises

Modern Critical Interpretations

The Oresteia
Beowulf
The General Prologue to
    The Canterbury Tales
The Pardoner's Tale
The Knight's Tale
The Divine Comedy
Exodus
Genesis
The Gospels
The Iliad
The Book of Job
Volpone
Doctor Faustus
The Revelation of St.
    John the Divine
The Song of Songs
Oedipus Rex
The Aeneid
The Duchess of Malfi
Antony and Cleopatra
As You Like It
Coriolanus
Hamlet
Henry IV, Part I
Henry IV, Part II
Henry V
Julius Caesar
King Lear
Macbeth
Measure for Measure
The Merchant of Venice
A Midsummer Night's
    Dream
Much Ado About
    Nothing
Othello
Richard II
Richard III
The Sonnets
Taming of the Shrew
The Tempest
Twelfth Night
The Winter's Tale
Emma
Mansfield Park
Pride and Prejudice
The Life of Samuel
    Johnson
Moll Flanders
Robinson Crusoe
Tom Jones
The Beggar's Opera
Gray's Elegy
Paradise Lost
The Rape of the Lock
Tristram Shandy
Gulliver's Travels

Evelina
The Marriage of Heaven
    and Hell
Songs of Innocence and
    Experience
Jane Eyre
Wuthering Heights
Don Juan
The Rime of the Ancient
    Mariner
Bleak House
David Copperfield
Hard Times
A Tale of Two Cities
Middlemarch
The Mill on the Floss
Jude the Obscure
The Mayor of
    Casterbridge
The Return of the Native
Tess of the D'Urbervilles
The Odes of Keats
Frankenstein
Vanity Fair
Barchester Towers
The Prelude
The Red Badge of
    Courage
The Scarlet Letter
The Ambassadors
Daisy Miller, The Turn
    of the Screw, and
    Other Tales
The Portrait of a Lady
Billy Budd, Benito Cer-
    eno, Bartleby the Scriv-
    ener, and Other Tales
Moby-Dick
The Tales of Poe
Walden
Adventures of
    Huckleberry Finn
The Life of Frederick
    Douglass
Heart of Darkness
Lord Jim
Nostromo
A Passage to India
Dubliners
A Portrait of the Artist as
    a Young Man
Ulysses
Kim
The Rainbow
Sons and Lovers
Women in Love
1984
Major Barbara

Man and Superman
Pygmalion
St. Joan
The Playboy of the
    Western World
The Importance of Being
    Earnest
Mrs. Dalloway
To the Lighthouse
My Antonia
An American Tragedy
Murder in the Cathedral
The Waste Land
Absalom, Absalom!
Light in August
Sanctuary
The Sound and the Fury
The Great Gatsby
A Farewell to Arms
The Sun Also Rises
Arrowsmith
Lolita
The Iceman Cometh
Long Day's Journey Into
    Night
The Grapes of Wrath
Miss Lonelyhearts
The Glass Menagerie
A Streetcar Named
    Desire
Their Eyes Were
    Watching God
Native Son
Waiting for Godot
Herzog
All My Sons
Death of a Salesman
Gravity's Rainbow
All the King's Men
The Left Hand of
    Darkness
The Brothers Karamazov
Crime and Punishment
Madame Bovary
The Interpretation of
    Dreams
The Castle
The Metamorphosis
The Trial
Man's Fate
The Magic Mountain
Montaigne's Essays
Remembrance of Things
    Past
The Red and the Black
Anna Karenina
War and Peace

These and other titles in preparation

Modern Critical Interpretations

Ernest Hemingway's
The Sun Also Rises

Edited and with an introduction by
Harold Bloom
Sterling Professor of the Humanities
Yale University

Chelsea House Publishers
NEW YORK ◇ PHILADELPHIA

813.5 ERN

10 9 8 7 6 5 4 3 2

∞ The paper used in this publication meets the minimum
requirements of the American National Standard for Permanence
of Paper for Printed Library Materials, Z39.48-1984.

Library of Congress Cataloging-in-Publication Data
Ernest Hemingway's The sun also rises.
   (Modern critical interpretations)
   Bibliography: p.
   Includes index.
   Summary: A collection of eleven critical essays on
Hemingway's novel "The Sun Also Rises" arranged in
chronological order of publication.
   1. Hemingway, Ernest, 1899–1961.   Sun also rises.
[1. Hemingway, Ernest, 1899–1961. Sun also rises.
2. American literature—History and criticism]
I. Bloom, Harold.   II. Series.
PS3515.E37Z586954   1987   813'.52   87–6342
ISBN 1–55546–053–4 (alk. paper)

Contents

Editor's Note / vii

Introduction / 1
    HAROLD BLOOM

The Wastelanders / 9
    CARLOS BAKER

The Death of Love in *The Sun Also Rises* / 25
    MARK SPILKA

Implications of Form in *The Sun Also Rises* / 39
    WILLIAM L. VANCE

Ernest Hemingway and the Rhetoric of Escape / 51
    ROBERT O. STEPHENS

Meyer Wolfsheim and Robert Cohn: A Study
of a Jewish Type and Stereotype / 61
    JOSEPHINE Z. KNOPF

Hemingway's Morality of Compensation / 71
    SCOTT DONALDSON

The End of *The Sun Also Rises:* A New Beginning / 91
    CAROLE GOTTLIEB VOPAT

The Sun Also Rises: One Debt to Imagism / 103
    LINDA W. WAGNER

False Dawn: *The Sun Also Rises* Manuscript / 117
    MICHAEL S. REYNOLDS

What's Funny in *The Sun Also Rises* / 133
    JAMES HINKLE

Toreo: The Moral Axis of *The Sun Also Rises* / 151
    ALLEN JOSEPHS

Chronology / 169

Contributors / 171

Bibliography / 173

Acknowledgments / 177

Index / 179

Editor's Note

I

This book gathers together a representative selection of the most helpful criticism yet published on Ernest Hemingway's novel *The Sun Also Rises*. The critical essays are reprinted here in the chronological order of their original publication. I am grateful to Susan Beegel for her aid in researching this volume, and to James Hinkle and Charles Oliver for their kind cooperation.

My introduction centers upon Hemingway's rhetorical stance, as the point where his style and sensibility come together. Carlos Baker, Hemingway's prime biographer, begins the chronological sequence of criticism with his portrait of the Lost Generation or Wastelanders who provided the historical context for *The Sun Also Rises*. It is followed here by Mark Spilka's now classical study of the sorrows of Eros in Hemingway's best novel.

William L. Vance emphasizes the formal unity (particularly of action) in the book, while Robert O. Stephens attempts to distinguish between true and false expatriates among the characters. The anti-Semitic stereotype of Robert Cohn (Hemingway angrily denied anti-Semitic intentions) is contrasted by Josephine Z. Knopf to that of the gambler Meyer Wolfsheim in Scott Fitzgerald's *The Great Gatsby*. Focusing upon various characters' attitudes toward money, Scott Donaldson inspects Hemingway's "faith in the efficacy and staying power of certain moral values."

In a meditation upon the novel's conclusion, Carole Gottlieb Vopat finds a significant change beginning in Jake Barnes, a view with which my introduction partly agrees, though it seems to me a necessarily hopeless fresh start. Linda W. Wagner reopens the question of the influence of Imagist poetry upon Hemingway's style in *The Sun*

Also Rises, while Michael S. Reynolds studies some of the relations between the completed novel and its manuscript origins.

In a useful cataloging of humor and verbal play in the novel, James Hinkle lovingly reminds us of some of the elements that first contributed to the impact of Hemingway's dialogue upon readers in the 1920s. This book concludes with Allen Joseph's passionate defense of Hemingway's vision of the matador as messiah, a defense that sums up much of the Spanish context of the book.

Introduction

Hemingway freely proclaimed his relationship to *Huckleberry Finn*, and there is some basis for the assertion, except that there is little in common between the rhetorical stances of Twain and of Hemingway. Kipling's *Kim*, in style and mode, is far closer to *Huckleberry Finn* than anything Hemingway wrote. The true accent of Hemingway's admirable style is to be found in an even greater and more surprising precursor:

> This grass is very dark to be from the white heads of old
>   mothers,
> Darker than the colorless beards of old men,
> Dark to come from under the faint red roofs of mouths.

Or again:

> I clutch the rails of the fence, my gore drips, thinn'd with
>   the ooze of my skin,
> I fall on the weeds and stones,
> The riders spur their unwilling horses, haul close,
> Taunt my dizzy ears and beat me violently over the head
>   with whip-stocks.
> Agonies are one of my changes of garments,
> I do not ask the wounded person how he feels, I myself
>   become the wounded person,
> My hurts turn livid upon me as I lean on a cane and observe.

Hemingway is scarcely unique in not acknowledging the paternity of Walt Whitman; T. S. Eliot and Wallace Stevens are far closer to Whitman than William Carlos Williams and Hart Crane were, but literary influence is a paradoxical and antithetical process, about which we continue to know all too little. The profound affinities between

Hemingway, Eliot, and Stevens are not accidental, but are family resemblances due to the repressed but crucial relation each had to Whitman's work. Hemingway characteristically boasted (in a letter to Sara Murphy, February 27, 1936) that he had knocked Stevens down quite handily: "for statistics sake Mr. Stevens is 6 feet 2 weighs 225 lbs. and . . . when he hits the ground it is highly spectaculous." Since this match between the two writers took place in Key West on February 19, 1936, I am moved, as a loyal Stevensian, for statistics' sake to point out that the victorious Hemingway was born in 1899, and the defeated Stevens in 1879, so that the novelist was then going on thirty-seven, and the poet verging on fifty-seven. The two men doubtless despised one another, but in the letter celebrating his victory, Hemingway calls Stevens "a damned fine poet" and Stevens always affirmed that Hemingway was essentially a poet, a judgment concurred in by Robert Penn Warren when he wrote that Hemingway "is essentially a lyric rather than a dramatic writer." Warren compared Hemingway to Wordsworth, which is feasible, but the resemblance to Whitman is far closer. Wordsworth would not have written: "I am the man, I suffer'd, I was there," but Hemingway almost persuades us he would have achieved that line had not Whitman set it down first.

II

It is now more than twenty years since Hemingway's suicide, and some aspects of his permanent canonical status seem beyond doubt. Only a few modern American novels seem certain to endure: *The Sun Also Rises, The Great Gatsby, Miss Lonelyhearts, The Crying of Lot 49,* and at least several by Faulkner, including *As I Lay Dying, Sanctuary, Light in August, The Sound and the Fury, Absalom, Absalom!* Two dozen stories by Hemingway could be added to the group, indeed perhaps all of *The First Forty-Nine Stories.* Faulkner is an eminence apart, but critics agree that Hemingway and Fitzgerald are his nearest rivals, largely on the strength of their shorter fiction. What seems unique is that Hemingway is the only American writer of prose fiction in this century who, as a stylist, rivals the principal poets: Stevens, Eliot, Frost, Hart Crane, aspects of Pound, W. C. Williams, Robert Penn Warren, and Elizabeth Bishop. This is hardly to say that Hemingway, at his best, fails at narrative or the representation of character. Rather, his peculiar excellence is closer to Whitman than to Twain, closer to Stevens than to Faulkner, and even closer to Eliot than to Fitzgerald, who was his friend and rival. He is an elegiac poet who mourns the self, who celebrates the self (rather less effectively), and who suffers divisions in the self. In the broadest tradition of American literature, he stems ultimately from the Emersonian reliance on the god within, which is the line of Whitman, Thoreau, and Dickinson. He arrives late and dark in this tradition, and is one of its negative theologians, as it were, but as in Stevens the negations, the cancellings, are never final. Even the most ferocious of his stories, say, "God Rest You Merry, Gentlemen" or "A Natural History of the Dead," can be said to celebrate what we might call the Real Absence. Doc Fischer, in "God Rest You Merry, Gentlemen," is a precursor of Nathanael West's Shrike in *Miss Lonelyhearts*, and his savage, implicit religiosity prophesies not only Shrike's Satanic stance but the entire demonic world of Pynchon's explicitly paranoid or Luddite visions. Perhaps there was a nostalgia for a Catholic order always abiding in Hemingway's consciousness, but the cosmos of his fiction, early and late, is American Gnostic, as it was in Melville, who first developed so strongly the negative side of the Emersonian religion of self-reliance.

III

Hemingway notoriously and splendidly was given to overtly agonistic images whenever he described his relationship to canonical writers, including Melville, a habit of description in which he has been followed by his true ephebe, Norman Mailer. In a grand letter (September 6–7, 1949) to his publisher, Charles Scribner, he charmingly confessed: "Am a man without any ambition, except to be champion of the world, I wouldn't fight Dr. Tolstoi in a 20 round bout because I know he would knock my ears off." This modesty passed quickly, to be followed by: "If I can live to 60 I can beat him. (MAYBE)" Since the rest of the letter counts Turgenev, Maupassant, Henry James, even Cervantes, as well as Melville and Dostoyevski, among the defeated, we can join Hemingway, himself, in admiring his extraordinary self-confidence. How justified was it, in terms of his ambitions?

It could be argued persuasively that Hemingway is the best short-story writer in the English language, from Joyce's *Dubliners* until the present. The aesthetic dignity of the short story need not be questioned, and yet we seem to ask more of a canonical writer. Hemingway wrote *The Sun Also Rises* and not *Ulysses*, which is only to say that his true genius was for very short stories, and hardly at all for extended narrative. Had he been primarily a poet, his lyrical gifts would have sufficed: we do not hold it against Yeats that his poems, not his plays, are his principal glory. Alas, neither Turgenev nor Henry James, neither Melville nor Mark Twain provide true agonists for Hemingway. Instead Maupassant is the apter rival. Of Hemingway's intensity of style in the briefer compass, there is no question, but even *The Sun Also Rises* reads now as a series of epiphanies, of brilliant and memorable vignettes.

Much that has been harshly criticized in Hemingway, particularly in *For Whom the Bell Tolls*, results from his difficulty in adjusting his gifts to the demands of the novel. Robert Penn Warren suggests that Hemingway is successful when his "system of ironies and understatements is coherent." When incoherent, then Hemingway's rhetoric fails as persuasion, which is to say, we read *To Have and Have Not* or *For Whom the Bell Tolls* and we are all too aware that the system of tropes is primarily what we are offered. Warren believes this not to be true of *A Farewell to Arms*, yet even the celebrated close of the novel seems now a worn understatement:

> But after I had got them out and shut the door and turned off the light it wasn't any good. It was like saying good-by to a statue. After a while I went out and left the hospital and walked back to the hotel in the rain.

Contrast this to the close of "Old Man at the Bridge," a story only two and a half pages long:

> There was nothing to do about him. It was Easter Sunday and the Fascists were advancing toward the Ebro. It was a gray overcast day with a low ceiling so their planes were not up. That and the fact that cats know how to look after themselves was all the good luck that old man would ever have.

The understatement continues to persuade here because the stoicism remains coherent and is admirably fitted by the rhetoric. A very short story concludes itself by permanently troping the mood of a particular moment in history. Vignette is Hemingway's natural mode, or call it hard-edged vignette: a literary sketch that somehow seems to be the beginning or end of something longer, yet truly is complete in itself. Hemingway's style encloses what ought to be unenclosed, so that the genre remains subtle yet trades its charm for punch. But a novel of three hundred and forty pages (*A Farewell to Arms*) which I have just finished reading again (after twenty years away from it) cannot sustain itself upon the rhetoric of vignette. After many understatements, too many, the reader begins to believe that he is reading a Hemingway imitator, like the accomplished John O'Hara, rather than the master himself. Hemingway's notorious fault is the monotony of repetition, which becomes a dulling litany in a somewhat less accomplished imitator like Nelson Algren, and sometimes seems self-parody when we must confront it in Hemingway.

Nothing is got for nothing, and a great style generates defenses in us, particularly when it sets the style of an age, as the Byronic Hemingway did. As with Byron, the color and variety of the artist's life becomes something of a veil between the work and our aesthetic apprehension of it. Hemingway's career included four marriages (and three divorces); service as an ambulance driver for the Italians in World War I (with an honorable wound); activity as a war correspondent in the Greek-Turkish War (1922), the Spanish Civil War (1937–39), the Chinese-Japanese War (1941), and the war against Hitler in Europe (1944–45). Add big-game hunting and fishing, and safaris, expatriation in France and Cuba, bullfighting, the Nobel Prize, and ultimate suicide in Idaho, and you have an absurdly implausible life, apparently lived in imitation of Hemingway's own fiction. The final effect of the work and the life together is not less than mythological, as it was with Byron, and with Whitman and with Oscar Wilde. Hemingway now is myth, and so is permanent as an image of American heroism, or perhaps more ruefully the American illusion of heroism. The best of Hemingway's work, the stories and *The Sun Also Rises*, are also a permanent part of the American mythology. Faulkner, Stevens, Frost, perhaps Eliot, and Hart Crane were stronger writers than Hemingway, but he alone in this American century has achieved the enduring status of myth.

IV

Rereading *The Sun Also Rises* provides a few annoyances, particularly if one is a Jewish literary critic and somewhat skeptical of Hemingway's vision of the matador as messiah. Romero seems to me about as convincing a representation as Robert Cohn; they are archetypes for Hemingway in 1926, but hardly for us sixty years after. Brett and Mike are period pieces also; Scott Fitzgerald did them better. But these are annoyances only; the novel is as fresh now as when I first read it in

1946 when I was sixteen. Like *The Great Gatsby*, *The Sun Also Rises* ages beautifully. Why? What are the qualities that save this novel from its own *mystique*, its self-intoxication with its own rhetorical stance? What does it share with Hemingway's best stories, like those in the fine collection *Winner Take Nothing* ?

A great style is itself necessarily a trope, a metaphor for a particular attitude towards reality. Hemingway's is an art of evocation, hardly a singular or original mode, except that Hemingway evokes by parataxis, in the manner of Whitman, or of much in the English Bible. This is parataxis with a difference, a way of utterance that plays at a withdrawal from all affect, while actually investing affect in the constancy of the withdrawal, a willing choice of the void as object, rather than be void of object, in Nietzschean terms. Not that Hemingway is spurred by Nietzsche, since Conrad is clearly the largest precursor of the author of *The Sun Also Rises*. The stance of Marlow in *Lord Jim* and *Heart of Darkness* is the closest analogue to Hemingway's own rhetorical stance in *The Sun Also Rises* and *A Farewell to Arms*.

Erich Auerbach and Angus Fletcher are among the notable modern critics who have illuminated the literary uses of parataxis. Fletcher lucidly summarizes parataxis as a syntactic parallel to the symbolic action of literature:

> This term implies a structuring of sentences such that they
> do not convey any distinctions of higher or lower order.
> "Order" here means intensity of interest, since what is more
> important usually gets the greater share of attention.

Fletcher, without implying childlike or primitive behavior, indicates the psychological meaning of parataxis as being related to "the piecemeal behavior of young children or primitive peoples." As Fletcher notes, this need not involve the defense Freud named as regression, because a paratactic syntax "displays ambiguity, suggesting that there is a rhythmic order even deeper in its organizing force than the syntactic order."

Hemingway's parataxis is worthy of the full-length studies it has not yet received. Clearly it is akin to certain moments in Huck Finn's narration, Walt Whitman's reveries, and even Wallace Stevens's most sustained late meditations, such as *The Auroras of Autumn*. John Hollander usefully compares it also to "an Antonioni shooting script—in the relation of dialogue and shots of landscape cut away to as a move in the dialogue itself, rather than as mere punctuation, and ultimately in the way in which dialogue and uninterpreted glimpse of scene

interpret each other." I take it that the refusal of emphasis, the maintaining of an even tonality of apparent understatement, is the crucial
manifestation of parataxis in Hemingway's prose style. Consider the
celebrated conclusion of *The Sun Also Rises*:

> Down-stairs we came out through the first-floor dining-
> room to the street. A waiter went for a taxi. It was hot and
> bright. Up the street was a little square with trees and grass
> where there were taxis parked. A taxi came up the street,
> the waiter hanging out at the side. I tipped him and told the
> driver where to drive, and got in beside Brett. The driver
> started up the street. I settled back. Brett moved close to
> me. We sat close against each other. I put my arm around
> her and she rested against me comfortably. It was very hot
> and bright, and the houses looked sharply white. We turned
> out onto the Gran Via.
>
> "Oh, Jake," Brett said, "we could have had such a damned
> good time together."
>
> Ahead was a mounted policeman in khaki directing traf-
> fic. He raised his baton. The car slowed suddenly pressing
> Brett against me.
>
> "Yes," I said. "Isn't it pretty to think so?"

The question of Jakes' impotence is more than relevant here. It is
well to remember Hemingway's description of authorial intention,
given in the interview with George Plimpton:

> Actually he had been wounded in quite a different way and
> his testicles were intact and not damaged. Thus he was
> capable of all normal feelings as a *man* but incapable of
> consummating them. The important distinction is that his
> wound was physical and not psychological and that he was
> not emasculated.

The even, understated tone at the end of *The Sun Also Rises*
depends upon a syntax that carries parataxis to what might have been
parodistic excess, if Hemingway's art were less deliberate. Sentences
such as "It was hot and bright" and the sly "He raised his baton" are
psychic images of lost consummation, but they testify also to Jake's
estrangement from the earlier intensities of his love for Brett. Reduced
by his betrayal of the matador-messiah to Brett's rapacity, Jake is last
heard in transition towards a less childlike, less primitive mode of

reality-testing: " 'Yes.' I said. 'Isn't it pretty to think so?' " One remembers Nietzsche's reflection that what we find words for is something we already despise in our hearts, so that there is always a sort of contempt in the act of speaking. Kenneth Burke, in *Counter-Statement*, rejoined that the contempt might be *in* the act, but not contempt *for* speaking. Jake, as the novel ends, is in transition towards Burke's position.

Hemingway possessed both a great style and an important sensibility. He was not an original moralist, a major speculative intellect, a master of narrative, or superbly gifted in the representation of persons. That is to say, he was not Tolstoy, whom he hoped to defeat he said, if only he could live long enough. But style and sensibility can be more than enough, as *The Sun Also Rises* demonstrates. Style alone will not do it; consider Updike or Cheever. We go back to *The Sun Also Rises* to learn a sensibility and to modify our own in the process of learning.

The Wastelanders

Carlos Baker

> *It is the mark of the true novelist that in searching the meaning of his own unsought experience, he comes on the moral history of his time.*
>
> JOHN PEALE BISHOP

BEAT-UP, NOT LOST

"Hemingway's first novel might rock the country," wrote Alfred Harcourt to Louis Bromfield one day in 1925. The prediction was sound. A year had not gone by before Hemingway awoke one autumn morning in Paris to find that the sun had also risen.

He had labored long and hard to give his first novel (really his third if you counted the one that was stolen and *The Torrents of Spring*) the solid structure and the freshness of texture which have since sustained it. "I started *The Sun Also Rises* on the 21st of July, my [26th] birthday, in Valencia," he wrote. Work on the first draft was continued through the last ten days of July and the month of August in Valencia, Madrid, St. Sebastian, and Hendaye, and the complete runthrough was finished in Paris on September 21, 1925.

"There is only one thing to do with a novel," he once told Fitzgerald, "and that is to go straight on through to the end of the damned thing." The remark was perhaps designed as an exhortation to Fitzgerald, whose dilatory habits in the completion of novels occasioned some pain to a friend who wished him well. The first draft of *The Sun Also Rises* was set down in approximately forty-eight writing days, but Hemingway nearly killed himself in the process. "I knew nothing about writing a novel when I started it," he recalled in 1948,

From *Hemingway: The Writer as Artist.* © 1956, 1963, 1972, 1980 by Carlos Baker. Princeton University Press, 1952.

"and so wrote too fast and each day to the point of complete exhaustion. So the first draft was very bad . . . I had to rewrite it completely. But in the rewriting I learned much."

Following a rest period during which he produced *The Torrents of Spring* and gave his first draft a chance to settle and objectify itself, he went down to Schruns in the Vorarlberg in mid-December. Here he spent the period before Christmas in skiing and revising his book. A trip to New York in mid-February provided a brief interlude in the concentrated labors of rewriting. These filled January, part of February, and the month of March. By April first the book was ready for the typist. Heavy cuts in the original opening and elsewhere had now reduced a much longer novel to about 90,000 words. The completed typescript was mailed to Maxwell Perkins on April 24, 1926. The total operation had covered nine months of extremely hard work.

The result justified the effort. If there had been any suspicion that Hemingway's skills were limited to short fiction, the publication of the first novel on October 22, 1926, dispelled it. The book showed, said a pleased reviewer, that he could state a theme dramatically and develop it to book length, a problem not previously attacked except for purposes of travesty in the book on Anderson. Three years later, on September 27, 1929, Hemingway proved with *A Farewell to Arms* that he could do it again. The interim publication of *Men without Women* (October 14, 1927) indicated that the novelist had not killed the short-story writer. But the books which elevated him to fame, and established him firmly on that eminence, were a pair of remarkable novels.

"Famous at twenty-five; thirty a master" was MacLeish's summary of the record. In their respective ways *The Sun Also Rises* and *A Farewell to Arms* also summarized a record. In reverse chronological order, they represented the essence of that densely packed period in Hemingway's life between 1918 and 1925. They struck a total for the meaning of his own experience, both sought and unsought, and became in effect two long chapters in the moral history of the nineteen-twenties.

No book is inevitable, though every good book comes out of a strong internal compulsion. Given a man of Hemingway's talents and experience, both books happened naturally. They were done not only for reasons of normal artistic compulsion but also as a means of trying-out the moral essence of seven years. If *The Torrents of Spring* was a declaration of esthetic independence, *The Sun Also Rises* was the means Hemingway chose to declare himself out of the alleged "lostness" of a generation whose vagaries he chronicled. In 1922 he had recorded his humorous scorn for the artistic scum of Montparnasse. Now, through Jake Barnes, he withdrew to the position of a detached observer looking on at aimless revels which at once amused him and left him sick at heart. For it is one view of Jake that he is an imperturbable and damaged Hamlet. By talking thus and thus at the court of the Duchess of the Dôme, he rids himself of a deep-seated disgust for the oppressions of his environment and the people who make it oppressive. In somewhat the same fashion, *A Farewell to Arms* meant the shunting-off of the old war, writing it out, getting rid of it by setting it down in all its true intermixture of humor and horror— until, thirty years after, the rude ceremonial of Colonel Cantwell on a grassed-over Italian battleground could bury it forever.

There was much more to these first two novels, of course, than an act of personal exorcism, however complicated. For to destroy by embodying is also to create by arranging. The artist's special blessing exists in the impulse to destroy an aspect of the thing he creates, and to render permanent what for him, in another and internal dimension, must be permanently destroyed. By 1929, Hemingway had done both tasks. With the attainment, at age thirty, of his majority as a writer, he became what he had not been so completely before—the free man who had served his apprenticeship to an art and fulfilled (in quite another way) his obligations to society. From that date on he moved off on another tack, and one began to catch echoes of one of his favored maxims: "Don't do anything too bloody long."

Of *The Sun Also Rises*, Robert Littell brightly remarked that it "won the *succès de scandale* of a *roman à clef* floated on *vin ordinaire*." An immediate cause of its success was that if one knew something about the Montparnassians who frequented the Dôme, the Rotonde, the Sélect, the Deux Magots, the Napolitain, the Dingo Bar, or Zelli's during the period 1923–25, one likewise possessed a key which would admit the bearer to the "real" identities of the fictional people. As Model-T jokes helped early Fords to fame, so the international guessing-game of who was who in *The Sun Also Rises* assisted with the word-of-mouth promotion of the book. The prototypes of Robert Cohn, Lady Brett Ashley, and Mike Campbell were all familiarly known in the Latin Quarter. Though Pedro Romero bore the name of an eighteenth-century matador, he was clearly a projection of Niño de la Palma in his great period before a series of bad horn-wounds damaged his nerve. Wielders of the key could, of course, unlock the identities of Bill

Gorton, Mr. and Mrs. Braddocks, Count Mippipopoulos, Wilson-Harris the Englishman at Burguete, or Robert Prentiss, the American novelist with the cultivated Oxford accent. For a time after the book was published, Paris gossip asserted that its title should have been *Six Characters in Search of an Author— With a Gun Apiece*. Still, as Hemingway pointed out to Fitzgerald, "no bullets whistled." When the *scandale* had run its course, the wise ones turned to a new topic of absorbing interest: which author had Hemingway imitated when he wrote *The Sun Also Rises*, Fitzgerald in *This Side of Paradise* or Michael Arlen in *The Green Hat?*

Littell had observed that many of the people had been "practically kidnapped" into Hemingway's novel. Such kidnapping, if that was the best descriptive term, was hardly a new experiment. Sherwood Anderson, starting with the actual residents of his Chicago boarding-house and allowing his mind to play freely over their supposed frustrations, had evolved a population for his *Winesburg, Ohio*. Lewis's *Main Street*, Fitzgerald's *This Side of Paradise*, or a little later Bravig Imbs's *The Professor's Wife* all had recognizable real-life sources. Among the poets, Frost, Robinson, and Masters invented in terms of people they knew. Yeats in the holy land of Ireland praised Maud Gonne into public property. People knew the background of Douglas's *South Wind*, Huxley's *Antic Hay*, and Joyce's *Portrait of the Artist as a Young Man*. It was, in fact, an age of indirect or direct "transcription," when the perfectly sound esthetic theory was that the author must invent out of his own experience or run the risk of making hollow men of his characters. Hemingway shared in the belief (which has been called behaviorist) that any group of living people, placed under the microscope and candidly watched for typical or idiosyncratic conduct, can be made to provide the groundwork of a novel.

The question with any such novel is always whether it has the power to survive the immediate moment when its possible real-life origins are being gossiped about. Unless the *clef* of a *roman à clef* is finally irrelevant, the novel can have no more just claim on the interest of posterity than the society pages or racing forms from last year's newspaper. The *succès de scandale* of 1926 could not possibly explain the rapidity and assurance with which *The Sun Also Rises* became, as it has remained, one of the genuine classics of modern American fiction.

Hemingway did not at all intend to have his novel construed as a textbook of lost-generationism. But the "Lost Generation" catchphrase, facing the title page, seemed to sum up for many people an aspect of the social history of the nineteen-twenties. Ernest Boyd said that Hemingway had triumphantly added a new chapter to the story Fitzgerald began in *This Side of Paradise*. The feeling was that both books, though in far different ways, helped to anatomize the desperate gaiety with which the Jazz Age covered its melancholia. And there can be no doubt that, with his brilliant dramatization of the moral predicament of a small group of Jazz Age D. P.'s, Hemingway offered a "myth" whose extension in social space far outreached the novel's national boundaries of France and Spain. What he had done could be regarded as dramatized social history. But it was not intended to be the social history of a lost generation.

Towards the materials of his book Hemingway's attitude was more complex than has since been generally understood. Because he quite properly refused to explain his position in other than dramatic terms, and because, in his dramatization, he would not consent to oversimplify, he was often taken for the sentimental and mournful singer of an empty day, or, quite as erroneously, as the hardshelled and disillusioned chronicler of social disintegration.

One illustration of the extent of the misunderstanding is the contrast which Hemingway intended to draw by giving the book its two epigraphs, one from Gertrude Stein and the other from Ecclesiastes. The remark there attributed to "Gertrude Stein in conversation" did not represent the position of Hemingway. According to his testimony, she said it in French, and it was supposed to have been said to her by "a garage-keeper in the Midi describing his mechanics, the young ones; *une génération perdue*." Gertrude Stein sought to extend the application of the remark from the young French mechanics (with their marked ineptitudes in the proper use of screwdrivers) to all the sad young men whom the late war and the high cost of living had cast up on the shores of France.

As Hemingway explained to Perkins on November 19, 1926, he regarded the "lost generation" comment as a piece of "splendid bombast" and was very skeptical of "Gertrude's assumption of prophetic roles." He could not agree with her at all. He himself did not feel lost. His reason for adding the quotation from Ecclesiastes was to indicate his own belief that "there was no such thing as a lost generation."

"I thought [he said in 1951] beat-up, maybe, [deleted] in many ways. But damned if we were lost except for deads, *gueules cassées*, and certified crazies. Lost, no. And Criqui, who was a real *gueule cassée*, won the featherweight championship of the world. We were a very solid generation though without education (some of us). But you could always get it.''

In order to write his book it had been necessary for Hemingway to dissociate himself in a moral sense from the very idea of lostness. He might tell Fitzgerald that *The Sun Also Rises* was "a hell of a sad story" whose only instruction was "how people go to hell." But the point of the book for him, as he wrote Perkins, was "that the earth abideth forever." He had "a great deal of fondness and admiration for the earth, and not a hell of a lot for my generation," and he cared "little about vanities." The book was not meant to be "a hollow or bitter satire, but a damn tragedy with the earth abiding forever as the hero."

The reading public in general did not appear to understand the point or the degree of dissociation between the artist and his characters. One heard that Jake Barnes was a modified self-portrait of Hemingway, dripping with self-pity, when in fact Hemingway was facing the hazards of *la vie humaine* with courage and a reasonably light heart, as, for that matter, was Jake Barnes. "There really is, to me anyway, very great glamour in life—and places and all sorts of things and I would like sometime to get it into the stuff," he wrote to Maxwell Perkins. "I've known some very wonderful people who even though they were going directly to the grave (which is what makes any story a tragedy if carried out until the end) managed to put up a very fine performance en route." It ought to have been plain to discerning readers that Jake Barnes, Bill Gorton, and Pedro Romero were solid—if slightly beat-up—citizens of the republic. They were not lost. They refused to surrender to neuroses like those which beset Robert Cohn, Brett Ashley, and Mike Campbell. And three lost neurotics do not make a lost generation.

It was one of the ironies that Hemingway, having rejected the lost-generation tag both for himself and for his generation, should find his first book widely accepted as Exhibit A of "lost-generationism." Another conspicuous irony was that most readers found Brett and her little circle of drinking-companions so fascinating as to overshadow the idea of the abiding earth as the true hero of the book. Hemingway's love and admiration for the natural earth was certainly quite clearly projected. Any beat-up Antaeus who could gain strength and sanity from contact with the earth was a kind of hero in his eyes, as one saw in the portraits of Barnes and Gorton and Romero. Yet all eyes were drawn towards Brett—possibly by the odd mixture of irony and pity, of condemnation and admiration, with which she was treated.

COUNTERPOINT

Hemingway had told Perkins that he cared little about the vanities. *The Sun Also Rises* was one of the proofs of that statement. The title comes from the first chapter of Ecclesiastes. It is useful to recognize the strong probability that the moral of the novel is derived from the same book: "All is vanity and vexation of spirit." All is vanity, at any rate, along the Vanity Fair of the Boulevard Montparnasse where the novelist introduces his people and completes his preliminary exposition. "Everybody's sick," says Jake's little *poule* in the Parisian horsecab. The novel goes on to prove that if you concentrate on a certain segment of expatriated society, she is very nearly right. All is vanity at the Pamplona fiesta when Cohn and Campbell, moody and sullen among the empty bottles, bicker over Brett while she makes off with the matador. All is vanity when Jake concludes this little chapter of social history in a taxi on the Gran Via of Madrid. "Oh, Jake," cries Brett, "we could have had such a damned good time together." "Yes," Jake answers, closing the volume. "Isn't it pretty to think so?"

The novel contains, however, enough bright metal to bring out by contrast the special darkness of the sullen ground. We are meant to understand that all is vanity—except the things that are not vain. The moral norm of the book is a healthy and almost boyish innocence of spirit, and it is carried by Jake Barnes, Bill Gorton, and Pedro Romero. Against this norm, in the central antithesis of the novel, is ranged the sick abnormal "vanity" of the Ashley-Campbell-Cohn triangle.

Long before the middle of the book, a reader who is reasonably sensitive to changes in tone may discover that he has been silently forced into a choice between two sets of moral and emotional atmospheres. Something tarnished is opposed to something bright; vanity is challenged by sanity; a world of mean and snarled disorder is set off against a world clear of entangling alliances. The whole mood of the novel brightens, for example, when the men-without-women, Jake Barnes and Bill Gorton, climb to the roof of the bus which will take them to Burguete in the Pyrenees. This bright mood has passed through certain preliminary stages. One is the pleasant dinner which the two friends have shared at Madame Lecomte's in Paris. Another comes when Bill and Jake entrain at the Gare d'Orsay for Bayonne. Almost immediately they are in the well-known eighteenth-century situation where every prospect pleases and only man is vile. Vile is hardly the word, of course, for all the people they meet. Certain fellow-travelers on the train, and later on the bus, admirably sustain their holiday mood. But their delight in "the country" and its quiet beauties, as seen from the train-windows, anticipates the Burguete experience.

If the reader performs the experiment of watching the country over the shoulders of the travelers, he is likely to be struck by the way in which the references to natural beauty are used to document the feeling of holiday (a holiday from the company of Brett and her friends) which Jake and Bill share. An otherwise unforgivable compression of the train-ride chapter will illustrate the point.

> It was a lovely day, not too hot, and the country was beautiful from the start. We went back to the diner and had breakfast. . . . [Later] we ate the sandwiches and drank the Chablis and watched the country out of the window. The grain was just beginning to ripen and the fields were full of poppies. The pastureland was green, and there were fine trees, and sometimes big rivers and chateaux off in the trees. . . . About seven-thirty we had dinner and watched the country through the open window of the diner. . . . It got dark and we could feel the country hot and sandy and dark outside of the window, and about nine o'clock we got into Bayonne. . . . It was a nice hotel, and the people at the desk were very cheerful, and we each had a good small room. . . . Bayonne is a nice town. It is like a very clean Spanish town and it is on a big river.

The chapter carefully establishes the beauty of the countryside and the healthy male companionship between Jake and Bill. What makes them happiest, though they do not say so, is their freedom from the petty and noxious tribulations of Robert Cohn and company.

Although they meet Cohn in Bayonne and drive with him to Pamplona, Bill and Jake have already established between them an unspoken camaraderie into which Cohn and his troubles do not greatly intrude. Across the Spanish frontier, for example, they come upon a handsome vista. "The road went on, very white and straight ahead, and then lifted to a little rise, and off on the left was a hill with an old castle, with buildings close around it and a field of grain going right up to the walls and shifting in the wind." Jake, who is riding in the front seat with the driver, turns around as if to comment on the scene.

"Robert Cohn was asleep, but Bill looked and nodded his head." No word is spoken, but the friendly shared reaction of Jake and Bill is silently and strongly affirmed. Cohn is asleep and out of it.

Being so much involved in his dream of Brett, Robert Cohn, the man not free of woman, refuses to take the Burguete bus with the good companions. Instead, by way of preparation for Brett's imminent arrival, he bathes carefully, gets a shave and haircut, has a shampoo and an application of pomade, fumes petulantly over Brett's failure to reach Pamplona on schedule (she has drunk too much somewhere to the north), and watches Bill and Jake depart for their fishing-trip without the pleasure of his company.

In Burguete, for five memorable days, all is gold. At that elevation the air is cool and bracing. The good companions walk happily over the uplands among the sturdy beech-trees, fish the clear brown streams, and recline in the lap of real country. This is what they were admiring, and silently longing for, during the train-trip from Paris to Bayonne. Jake digs for worms in the grassy bank; they catch trout; they eat rustic lunches of wine and sandwiches in the good air. At night they play three-handed bridge with the English sportsman Wilson-Harris. There is much playful and boy-like badinage. The landscape smiles, as healthful and vitalizing as ever the English Lake District was in Wordsworth. Somewhere in the remote background, out of sight and as far out of mind as possible, is the Ashley-Campbell-Cohn triangle. The comrades are not troubled. For a brief but golden age there is "no word from Robert Cohn nor from Brett and Mike."

Hemingway's careful contrast of emotional and social climates makes the prefatory quotation from Ecclesiastes directly relevant. "One generation passeth away," says the preacher, "and another generation cometh; but the earth abideth for ever." Wherever they go, Brett and her little coterie (the truly "lost" part of that otherwise unlost generation) carry along with them the neuroses of Montparnasse. But the earth fortunately abides. The sun rises and sets over the fields and woods of France and Spain. The fresh winds blow; the rivers run in the valleys; the white roads ascend the mountains. For those who will look at it, all this is available. But the wastelanders pass away and out of the picture, and there is no health in them.

This pleasurable contrapuntal method, with its subtly marked contrast of emotional and moral climates, continues into the climactic phase of the novel. Now, however, there is a new image to take the place of Burguete. When the Pamplona fiesta begins, the light (and the lightheartedness) which the fishermen have known in the Pyrenees grows dim and comes very near to going out. All the sullen jealousies and cross-purposes which Brett's presence causes are released among the vacationers. Outward signs of the venom which works within are Jake's obvious disgust at Cohn's fawning over Brett; Mike's relentless verbal bludgeoning of Cohn; and Cohn's physical bludgeoning of Mike and Jake. As if Brett's own neurosis were somehow communicable, her semi-voluntary victims writhe and snarl. All is vanity at Pamplona as it was in the Montparnasse cafés before the trip was undertaken.

For the Pamplona episodes the contrasting bright metal is not nature but rather a natural man, the brave matador Romero. He is used as a force of antithesis, manly, incorruptible, healthy, courageous, of complete integrity and self-possession. Beside him Mike seems a poor player indeed, and he conspicuously embodies the qualities which Cohn lacks. His control accents Cohn's emotionalism; his courage, Cohn's essential cowardice; his self-reliance, Cohn's miserable fawning dependence; his dignity, Cohn's self-pity; his natural courtesy, Cohn's basic rudeness and egotism.

The enmity between the bullfighter and the boxer—for the very nature of Romero abhors the moral vacuum in Cohn—reaches its climax when Cohn invades Romero's room and finds Brett there. In a bedroom fistfight the boxer has every advantage over the bullfighter except in those internal qualities which fists cannot touch. Though he is knocked down fifteen times, Romero will not lose consciousness, give up, shake hands, or stop trying to hit Cohn for as long as he can see him. Afterwards, like a Greek chorus, Bill and Mike close the chronicle-history of Robert Cohn, the pomaded sulker in the tent, and Romero, the manly and unspoiled warrior. "That's quite a kid," says Bill. "He ruined Cohn," says Mike. Cohn presently leaves Pamplona under the cloud of his own ruination. Romero's face may be cut up, but his moral qualities have triumphed, as they do again in the bullring the day following the brawl. He has been "beat-up" like many other members of his generation. But not "lost."

Maxwell Perkins, a good and perceptive editor, understood the intent of the novel perfectly. He admiringly called it "a healthy book, with marked satirical implications upon novels which are not— sentimentalized, subjective novels, marked by sloppy hazy thought." Its morality, like its esthetics, was notably healthy. Against the background of international self-seekers like Cohn, the true moral norm of the book (Bill and Jake at Burguete, Romero at Pamplona) stood out in high and shining relief.

CIRCE AND COMPANY

Hemingway's first novel provides an important insight into the special "mythological" methods which he was to employ with increasing assurance and success in the rest of his major writing. It is necessary to distinguish Hemingway's method from such "mythologizing" as that of Joyce in *Ulysses*, or Eliot in *The Waste Land*. For Hemingway early devised and subsequently developed a mythologizing tendency of his own which does not depend on antecedent literatures, learned footnotes, or the recognition of spot passages. *The Sun Also Rises* is a first case in point.

It might be jocularly argued, for example, that there is much more to the portrait of Lady Brett Ashley than meets the non-Homeric eye. It is very pleasant to think of the Pallas Athene, sitting among the statuary in one of her temples like Gertrude Stein among the Picassos in the rue de Fleurus, and murmuring to the Achaeans, homeward bound from the battle of Troy: "You are all a lost generation." As for Brett, Robert Cohn calls her Circe. "He claims she turns men into swine," says Mike Campbell. "Damn good. I wish I were one of these literary chaps." If Hemingway had been writing about brilliant literary chaps in the manner, say, of Aldous Huxley in *Chrome Yellow*, he might have undertaken to develop Cohn's parallel. It would not have been farther-fetched than Joyce's use of the Daedalus legend in *A Portrait of the Artist* or Eliot's kidnapping of Homeric Tiresias to watch over the mean little seductions of *The Waste Land*.

Was not Brett Ashley, on her low-lying island in the Seine, just such a fascinating peril as Circe on Aeaea? Did she not open her doors to all the modern Achaean chaps? When they drank her special potion of French applejack or Spanish wine, did they not become as swine, or in the modern idiom, wolves? Did not Jake Barnes, that wily Odysseus, resist the shameful doom which befell certain of his less wary comrades who became snarling beasts?

There are even parallel passages. Says Jake Barnes, thinking of Brett: "I lay awake thinking and my mind jumping around. . . . Then all of a sudden I started to cry. Then after a while it was better . . . and then I went to sleep." Says Ulysses on Aeaea: "My spirit was broken within me and I wept as I sat on the bed. . . . But when I had my fill of weeping and writhing, I made answer." Or what shall be made of Robert Cohn, quietly and classically asleep on the winecasks in the back room of a Pamplona tavern, wreathed with twisted garlics and dead to the world while Brett and the others carouse in the room beyond? "There was one named Elpenor," says the *Odyssey*, "the youngest of all; not very valiant in war nor sound of understanding, who had laid him down apart from his comrades in the sacred house of Circe, seeking the cool air, for he was heavy with wine. He heard the noise and bustle of his comrades as they moved about."

If he had wished to follow the mythological method of Eliot's *Waste Land* or Joyce's *Ulysses*, Hemingway could obviously have done so. But his own esthetic opinions carried him away from the literary kind of myth-adaptation and over into that deeper area of psychological symbol-building which does not require special literary equipment to be interpreted. One needs only sympathy and a few degrees of heightened emotional awareness. The special virtue of this approach to the problem of literary communication is that it can be grasped by all men and women because they are human beings. None of the best writers are without it. It might even be described as the residuum of "natural knowledge" and belief, visible in every artist after the traditional elements have been siphoned off. This is perhaps roughly what Keats meant by saying that Shakespeare led a life of allegory, his works being the comments on it. Thoreau's phrase for the same thing, as R. L. Cook has pointed out, is "dusky knowledge." Pilar, the Cumaean sybil of *For Whom the Bell Tolls*, moves regularly in this half-subliminal area. She inherits her skill and discernment from Hemingway.

Under the matter-of-factness of the account of the feria of San Fermin a sabidurían symbolism is at work. It does not become formally apparent until the party has assembled to prepare for the festival. Then, in several ways, it develops as a dialectical struggle between paganism and Christian orthodoxy—a natural and brilliant use of the fact that the fiesta is both secular and religious, and that the *riau-riau* dancers unabashedly follow the procession which bears the patron saint through the streets of Pamplona.

The contrast is admirably dramatized through Jake and Brett. Without apology or explanation, Jake Barnes is a religious man. As a professing Catholic, he attends masses at the cathedral before and during fiesta week. On the Saturday before the festival opens, Brett accompanies him. "She said she wanted to hear me go to confession," says Jake, "but I told her that not only was it impossible but it was not as interesting as it sounded, and, besides, it would be in a language she did not know." Jake's remark can be taken doubly. The language Brett does not know is Latin; it is also Spanish; but it is especially the language of the Christian religion. When she goes soon afterwards to have her fortune told at a gypsy camp, Brett presumably hears language that she *can* understand.

Her true symbolic colors are broken out on Sunday afternoon. She is in the streets with Jake watching the religious procession in which the image of San Fermin is translated from one church to another. Ahead of the formal procession and behind it are the *riau-riau* dancers. When Jake and Brett try to enter the chapel they are stopped at the door, ostensibly because she has no hat. But for one sufficiently awake to the ulterior meaning of the incident it strikingly resembles the attempt of a witch to gain entry into a Christian sanctum. Brett's witch-hood is immediately underscored. Back in the street she is encircled by the chanting pagan dancers who prevent her from joining their figure: "They wanted her as an image to dance around." When the song ends, she is rushed to a wineshop and seated on an up-ended wine-cask. The shop is dark and full of men singing,—"hard-voiced singing."

The intent of this episode is quite plain. Brett would not understand the language used in Christian confessional. She is forbidden to follow the religious procession into the chapel. The dancers adopt her as a pagan image. She is perfectly at home on the wine-cask amidst the hard-voiced singing of the nonreligious celebrants. Later in fiesta week the point is reemphasized. Jake and Brett enter the San Fermin chapel so that Brett can pray for Romero's success in the final bullfight of the celebration. "After a little," says Jake, "I felt Brett stiffen beside me, and saw she was looking straight ahead." Outside the chapel Brett explains what Jake has already guessed: "I'm damned bad for a religious atmosphere. I've got the wrong type of face."

She has, indeed. Her face belongs in wide-eyed concentration over the Tarot pack of Madame Sosostris, or any equivalent soothsayer in the gypsy camp outside Pamplona. It is perfectly at home in the center of the knot of dancers in the street or in the tavern gloom above the wine-cask. For Brett in her own way is a lamia with a British accent, a Morgan le Fay of Paris and Pamplona, the reigning queen of a paganized wasteland with a wounded fisher-king as her half-cynical squire. She is, rolled into one, the *femme fatale de trente ans damnée*. Yet she is always and conspicuously herself. The other designations are purely arbitrary labels which could be multiplied as long as one's list of enchantresses could be made to last. They are not necessary to the full symbolic meaning which Brett has in her own right and by virtue (if that is the word) of what she is made to do in the book.

Although Hemingway carefully skirts the moralistic, as his artistic beliefs require, the moral drift of the symbolic story is unmistakable. Shortly after *The Sun Also Rises* appeared, he remarked, as he had never overtly done in the book, that "people aren't all as bad as some writers find them or as hollowed out and exhausted emotionally as some of the *Sun* generation." The restriction was conspicuous. He did not say, "the lost generation." He said rather, "some of the *Sun* generation." His indictment, put into dramatic terms, was directed against those who allowed themselves to flounder in an emulsion of ennui and alcohol when there was so much else to be done, whether one was a championship-winning *gueule cassée* like Criqui or an ordinary citizen like Jake, engaged in readjusting himself to peacetime living. In contrast to the "hollow men" who went off the stage with something resembling a whimper, Hemingway presented another set of men who kept their mouths shut and took life as it came.

The emotional exhaustion of "some of the *Sun* generation" is accentuated by the oppositions Hemingway provides. Obviously no accidental intruder in the book is Romero, standing out in youthful dignity and strength against the background of displaced wastrels among whom Jake moves. The same is true of the interlude at Burguete, with Jake and Bill happily disentangled from the wastelanders, as if in wordless echo of Eliot's line: "In the mountains, there you feel free." However fascinating Brett and Cohn and Mike may be as freewheeling international adventurers, the book's implicit attitude is one of quizzical condemnation towards these and all their kind.

Despite this fact, one finds in the presentation of Brett Ashley an almost Jamesian ambiguity. It is as if the objective view of Brett were intentionally relieved by that kind of chivalry which is never wholly missing from the work of Hemingway. On the straight narrative plane the book appears to offer a study of a war-frustrated love affair between Brett and Jake. Brett's Circean characteristics are only partly responsible for the sympathy with which she is treated, though all enchantresses from Spenser's Acrasia to Coleridge's Geraldine are literally fascinating and Brett is no exception. Whenever Jake takes a long objective view of Lady Ashley, however, he is too honest not to see her for what she objectively is, an alcoholic nymphomaniac. To Cohn's prying questions about her, early in the book, Jake flatly answers: "She's a drunk."

There is, nevertheless, a short history behind her alcoholism and her constant restless shifting from male to male. During the war she was an assistant nurse; her own true love died; she married a psychotic British baronet who maltreated her; and at the time of the book she is waiting for a divorce decree in order to marry the playboy Mike Campbell. Furthermore—and this fact calls forth whatever chivalry one finds—she is in love with Jake, though both of them realize the hopelessness of the situation. She has not, as her fiancé observes, had an absolutely happy life, and Jake is prepared to take this into account when he judges her character. "Don't you know about Irony and Pity?" asks Bill Gordon during a verbal bout at Burguete. Jake knows all about them. They are the combination he uses whenever he thinks about Brett.

One of the ironies in the portrait of Brett is her ability to appreciate quality in the circle of her admirers. After the trip to San Sebastian with Robert Cohn she quickly rejects him. She does not do so sluttishly, merely in order to take up with another man, but rather for what to her is the moral reason that he is unmanly. Towards her fiancé Mike Campbell the attitude is somewhere in the middle ground of amused acceptance. He is Brett's sort, a good drinking companion living on an income nearly sufficient to allow him a perpetual holiday. "He's so damned nice and he's so awful," says Brett. "He's my sort of thing." Even though Brett can be both nice and awful with her special brand of ambiguity, she does save her unambiguous reverence for two men. One is the truly masculine Jake, whose total sexual disability has not destroyed his manhood. The other is Romero, whose sexual ability is obviously a recommendation but is by no means his only claim to admiration. It is finally to Brett's credit, and the measure of her appreciation of quality, that she sends Romero back to the bullring instead of destroying him as she might have done. This is no *belle dame sans merci*. She shows mercy both to her victim and to the remaining shreds of her self-respect.

The Heloisa-Abelard relationship of Brett and Jake is Hemingway's earliest engagement of an ancient formula—the sacrifice of Venus on the altar of Mars. In one way or another, the tragic fact of war or the aftereffects of social disruption tend to inhibit and betray the normal course of love, not only in *The Sun Also Rises* but also in *A*

Farewell to Arms, To Have and Have Not, The Fifth Column, For Whom the Bell Tolls, and *Across the River and into the Trees.* Brett, the first of the victims, is a kind of dark Venus. If she had not lost her "true love" in the late war, or if Jake's wound had not permanently destroyed his ability to replace the lost lover, Brett's progressive self-destruction would not have become the inevitable course it now appears to be.

Much of the continuing power of *The Sun Also Rises* comes from its sturdy moral backbone. The portraits of Brett Ashley and Robert Cohn, like that of their antithesis Romero, are fully and memorably drawn. A further and deep-lying cause of the novel's solidity is the subtle operative contrast between vanity and sanity, between paganism and orthodoxy, between the health and humor of Burguete and the sick neuroses of the Montparnassian ne'er do-wells. Other readers can value the book for the still-fresh representation of "the way it was" in Paris and Pamplona, Bayonne and Burguete, during the now nostalgically remembered middle twenties. Yet much of the final strength of *The Sun Also Rises* may be attributed to the complicated interplay between the two points of view which it embodies. According to one of them, the novel is a romantic study in sexual and ultimately in spiritual frustration. Beside this more or less orthodox view, however, must be placed the idea that it is a qualitative study of varying degrees of physical and spiritual manhood, projected against a background of ennui and emotional exhaustion which is everywhere implicitly condemned.

The Death of Love
in *The Sun Also Rises*

Mark Spilka

> *She turns and looks a moment in the glass,*
> *Hardly aware of her departed lover;*
> *Her brain allows one half-formed thought to pass:*
> *"Well now that's done: and I'm glad it's over."*
> *When lovely woman stoops to folly and*
> *Paces about her room again, alone,*
> *She smoothes her hair with automatic hand,*
> *And puts a record on the gramophone.*
> > T. S. ELIOT, *The Waste Land*

One of the most persistent themes of the twenties was the death of love in World War I. All the major writers recorded it, often in piecemeal fashion, as part of the larger postwar scene; but only Hemingway seems to have caught it whole and delivered it in lasting fictional form. His intellectual grasp of the theme might account for this. Where D. H. Lawrence settles for the shock of war on the Phallic Consciousness, or where Eliot presents assorted glimpses of sterility, Hemingway seems to design an extensive parable. Thus, in *The Sun Also Rises*, his protagonists are deliberately shaped as allegorical figures: Jake Barnes and Brett Ashley are two lovers desexed by the war; Robert Cohn is the false knight who challenges their despair; while Romero, the stalwart bullfighter, personifies the good life which will survive their failure. Of course, these characters are not abstractions in the text; they are realized through the most concrete style in American

From *Twelve Original Essays on Great American Novels*, edited by Charles Shapiro. © 1958 by Wayne State University Press.

fiction, and their larger meaning is implied only by their response to immediate situations. But the implications are there, the parable is at work in every scene, and its presence lends unity and depth to the whole novel.

Barnes himself is a fine example of this technique. Cut off from love by a shell wound, he seems to suffer from an undeserved misfortune. But as most readers agree, his condition represents a peculiar form of emotional impotence. It does not involve distaste for the flesh, as with Lawrence's crippled veteran, Clifford Chatterley; instead Barnes lacks the power to control love's strength and durability. His sexual wound, the result of an unpreventable "accident" in the war, points to another realm where accidents can always happen and where Barnes is equally powerless to prevent them. In book 2 of the novel he makes this same comparison while describing one of the dinners at Pamplona: "It was like certain dinners I remember from the war. There was much wine, an ignored tension, and a feeling of things coming that you could not prevent happening." This fear of emotional consequences is the key to Barnes's condition. Like so many Hemingway heroes, he has no way to handle subjective complications, and his wound is a token for this kind of impotence.

It serves the same purpose for the expatriate crowd in Paris. In some figurative manner these artists, writers, and derelicts have all been rendered impotent by the war. Thus, as Barnes presents them, they pass before us like a parade of sexual cripples, and we are able to measure them against his own forbearance in the face of a common problem. Whoever bears his sickness well is akin to Barnes; whoever adopts false postures, or willfully hurts others, falls short of his example. This is the organizing principle in book 1, this alignment of characters by their stoic qualities. But stoic or not, they are all incapable of love, and in their sober moments they seem to know it.

For this reason they feel especially upset whenever Robert Cohn appears. Cohn still upholds a romantic view of life, and since he affirms it with stubborn persistence, he acts like a goad upon his wiser contemporaries. As the narrator, Barnes must account for the challenge he presents them and the decisive turn it takes in later chapters. Accordingly, he begins the book with a review of Cohn's boxing career at Princeton. Though he has no taste for it, college boxing means a lot to Cohn. For one thing, it helps to compensate for anti-Semitic treatment from his classmates. More subtly, it turns him into an armed romantic, a man who can damage others in defense of his own beliefs. He also loves the pose of manhood which it affords him and seems strangely pleased when his nose is flattened in the ring. Soon other tokens of virility delight him, and he often confuses them with actual manliness. He likes the idea of a mistress more than he likes his actual mistress; or he likes the authority of editing and the prestige of writing, though he is a bad editor and a poor novelist. In other words, he always looks for internal strength in outward signs and sources. On leaving Princeton, he marries "on the rebound from the rotten time . . . in college." But in five years the marriage falls through, and he rebounds again to his present mistress, the forceful Frances Clyne. Then, to escape her dominance and his own disquiet, he begins to look for romance in far-off countries. As with most of his views, the source of this idea is an exotic book:

> He had been reading W. H. Hudson. That sounds like an innocent occupation, but Cohn had read and reread "The Purple Land." "The Purple Land" is a very sinister book if read too late in life. It recounts splendid imaginary amorous adventures of a perfect English gentleman in an intensely romantic land, the scenery of which is very well described. For a man to take it at thirty-four as a guidebook to what life holds is about as safe as it would be for a man of the same age to enter Wall Street direct from a French convent, equipped with a complete set of the more practical Alger books. Cohn, I believe, took every word of "The Purple Land" as literally as though it had been an R. G. Dun report.

Cohn's romanticism explains his key position in the parable. He is the last chivalric hero, the last defender of an outworn faith, and his function is to illustrate its present folly—to show us, through the absurdity of his behavior, that romantic love is dead, that one of the great guiding codes of the past no longer operates. "You're getting damned romantic," says Brett to Jake at one point in the novel. "No, bored," he replies, because for this generation boredom has become more plausible than love. As a foil to his contemporaries, Cohn helps to reveal why this is so.

Of course, there is much that is traditional in the satire on Cohn. Like the many victims of romantic literature, from Don Quixote to Tom Sawyer, he lives by what he reads and neglects reality at his own and others' peril. But Barnes and his friends have no alternative to

Cohn's beliefs. There is nothing here, for example, like the neat balance between sense and sensibility in Jane Austen's world. Granted that Barnes is sensible enough, that he sees life clearly and that we are meant to contrast his private grief with Cohn's public suffering, his self-restraint with Cohn's deliberate self-exposure. Yet, emasculation aside, Barnes has no way to measure or control the state of love; and though he recognizes this with his mind and tries to act accordingly, he seems no different from Cohn in his deepest feelings. When he is alone with Brett, he wants to live with her in the country, to go with her to San Sebastian, to go up to her room, to keep her in his own room, or to keep on kissing her—though he can never really act upon such sentiments. Nor are they merely the yearnings of a tragically impotent man, for eventually they will lead Barnes to betray his own principles and to abandon self-respect, all for the sake of Lady Ashley. No, at best he is a restrained romantic, a man who carries himself well in the face of love's impossibilities, but who seems to share with Cohn a common (if hidden) weakness.

The sexual parade continues through the early chapters. Besides Cohn and his possessive mistress, there is the prostitute Georgette, whom Barnes picks up one day "because of a vague sentimental idea that it would be nice to eat with some one." Barnes introduces her to his friends as his fiancée, and as his private joke affirms, the two have much in common. Georgette is sick and sterile, having reduced love to a simple monetary exchange; but like Barnes, she manages to be frank and forthright and to keep an even keel among the drifters of Paris. Together they form a pair of honest cripples, in contrast with the various pretenders whom they meet along the Left Bank. Among the latter are Cohn and Frances Clyne, the writer Braddocks and his wife, and Robert Prentiss, a rising young novelist who seems to verbalize their phoniness: "Oh, how charmingly you get angry," he tells Barnes. "I wish I had that faculty." Barnes's honest anger has been aroused by the appearance of a band of homosexuals, accompanied by Brett Ashley. When one of the band spies Georgette, he decides to dance with her; then one by one the rest follow suit, in deliberate parody of normal love. Brett herself provides a key to the dizzy sexual medley. With a man's felt hat on her boyish bob, and with her familiar reference to men as fellow "chaps," she completes the distortion of sexual roles which seems to characterize the period. For the war, which has unmanned Barnes and his contemporaries, has turned Brett into the freewheeling equal of any man. It has taken her first sweetheart's life through dysentery and has sent her present husband home in a dangerous state of shock. For Brett these blows are the equivalent of Jake's emasculation; they seem to release her from her womanly nature and expose her to the male prerogatives of drink and promiscuity. Once she claims these rights as her own, she becomes an early but more honest version of Catherine Barkley, the English nurse in Hemingway's next important novel, *A Farewell to Arms*. Like Catherine, Brett has been a nurse on the Italian front and has lost a sweetheart in the war; but for her there is no saving interlude of love with a wounded patient, no rigged and timely escape through death in childbirth. Instead she survives the colossal violence, the disruption of her personal life, and the exposure to mass promiscuity, to confront a moral and emotional vacuum among her postwar lovers. With this evidence of male default all around her, she steps off the romantic pedestal, moves freely through the bars of Paris, and stands confidently there beside her newfound equals. Ironically, her most recent conquest, Robert Cohn, fails to see the bearing of such changes on romantic love. He still believes that Brett is womanly and therefore deeply serious about intimate matters. After their first meeting, he describes her as "absolutely fine and straight" and nearly strikes Barnes for thinking otherwise; and a bit later, after their brief affair in the country, he remains unconvinced "that it didn't mean anything." But when men no longer command respect, and women replace their natural warmth with masculine freedom and mobility, there can be no serious love.

Brett does have some respect for Barnes, even a little tenderness, though her actions scarcely show abiding love. At best she can affirm his worth and share his standards and perceptions. When in public, she knows how to keep her essential misery to herself; when alone with Barnes, she will express her feelings, admit her faults, and even display good judgment. Thus her friend, Count Mippipopolous, is introduced to Barnes as "one of us." The count qualifies by virtue of his war wounds, his invariable calmness, and his curious system of values. He appreciates good food, good wine, and a quiet place in which to enjoy them. Love also has a place in his system, but since he is "always in love," the place seems rather shaky. Like Jake and Brett and perhaps Georgette, he simply bears himself well among the postwar ruins.

The count completes the list of cripples who appear in book 1. In a broader sense, they are all disaffiliates, all men and women who have cut themselves off from conventional society and who have made Paris their permanent playground. Jake Barnes has introduced them, and we have been able to test them against his stoic attitudes toward life in a moral wasteland. Yet such life is finally unbearable, as we have also seen whenever Jake and Brett are alone together, or whenever Jake is alone with his thoughts. He needs a healthier code to live by, and for this reason the movement in book 2 is away from Paris to the trout stream at Burguete and the bullring at Pamplona. Here a more vital testing process occurs, and with the appearance of Bill Gorton, we get our first inkling of its nature.

Gorton is a successful writer who shares with Barnes a love for boxing and other sports. In Vienna he has helped to rescue a splendid Negro boxer from an angry and intolerant crowd. The incident has spoiled Vienna for him, and as his reaction suggests, the sports world will provide the terms of moral judgment from this point onward in the novel. Or more accurately, Jake Barnes's feelings about sports will shape the rest of the novel. For with Hemingway, the great outdoors is chiefly a state of mind, a projection of moral and emotional attitudes onto physical arenas, so that a clear account of surface action will reproduce these attitudes in the reader. In "Big Two-Hearted River," for example, he describes Nick Adams's fishing and camping activities along a trout stream in Michigan. His descriptions run to considerable length, and they are all carefully detailed, almost as if they were meant for a fishing manual. Yet the details themselves have strong emotional connotations for Nick Adams. He thinks of his camp as "the good place," the place where none of his previous troubles can touch him. He has left society behind him, and as the story begins, there is even a burnt town at his back, to signify his disaffiliation. He has also walked miles to reach an arbitrary campsite, and this is one of the ways in which he sets his own conditions for happiness and then lives up to them. He finds extraordinary pleasure, moreover, in the techniques of making coffee and pitching camp, or in his responses to fishing and eating. In fact, his sensations have become so valuable that he doesn't want to rush them: they bring health, pleasure, beauty, and a sense of order which is sorely missing in his civilized experience; they are part of a healing process, a private and imaginative means of wiping out the damages of civilized life. When this process is described with elaborate attention to surface detail, the effect on the reader is decidedly subjective.

The same holds true, of course, for the fishing trip in *The Sun Also Rises*. As Barnes and Gorton approach "the good place," each item in the landscape is singled out and given its own importance.

Later the techniques of fishing are treated with the same reverence for detail. For like Nick Adams, these men have left the wasteland for the green plains of health; they have traveled miles, by train and on foot, to reach a particular trout stream. The fishing there is good, the talk free and easy, and even Barnes is able to sleep well after lunch, though he is usually an insomniac. The meal itself is handled like a mock religious ceremony: "Let us rejoice in our blessings," says Gorton. "Let us utilize the fowls of the air. Let us utilize the produce of the vine. Will you utilize a little, brother?" A few days later, when they visit the old monastery at Roncevalles, this combination of fishing, drinking, and male camaraderie is given an edge over religion itself. With their English friend, Harris, they honor the monastery as a remarkable place, but decide that "it isn't the same as fishing"; then all agree to "utilize" a little pub across the way. At the trout stream, moreover, romantic love is given the same comparative treatment and seems sadly foolish before the immediate joys of fishing:

> It was a little past noon and there was not much shade, but I sat against the trunk of two of the trees that grew together, and read. The book was something by A. E. W. Mason, and I was reading a wonderful story about a man who had been frozen in the Alps and then fallen into a glacier and disappeared, and his bride was going to wait twenty-four years exactly for his body to come out on the moraine, while her true love waited too, and they were still waiting when Bill came up [with four trout in his bag]. . . . His face was sweaty and happy.

As these comparisons show, the fishing trip has been invested with unique importance. By sticking closely to the surface action, Barnes has evoked the deeper attitudes which underlie it and which make it a therapeutic process for him. He describes himself now as a "rotten Catholic" and speaks briefly of his thwarted love for Brett; but with religion defunct and love no longer possible, he can at least find happiness through private and imaginative means. Thus he now constructs a more positive code to follow: as with Nick Adams, it brings him health, pleasure, beauty and order, and helps to wipe out the damage of his troubled life in Paris.

Yet somehow the code lacks depth and substance. To gain these advantages, Barnes must move to Pamplona, which stands roughly to Burguete as the swamp in "Big Two-Hearted River" stands to the trout stream. In the latter story, Nick Adams prefers the clear portion of the river to its second and more congested heart:

> In the swamp the banks were bare, the big cedars came together overhead, the sun did not come through, except in patches; in the fast deep water, in the half light, the fishing would be tragic. In the swamp fishing was a tragic adventure. Nick did not want it. . . . There were plenty of days coming when he could fish the swamp.

The fishing is tragic here because it involves the risk of death. Nick is not yet ready for that challenge, but plainly it will test his manhood when he comes to face it. In *The Sun Also Rises* Barnes makes no such demands upon himself; but he is strongly attracted to the young bullfighter, Pedro Romero, whose courage before death lends moral weight to the sportsman's code.

So Pamplona is an extension of Burguete for Barnes: gayer and more festive on the surface, but essentially more serious. The spoilers from Paris have arrived, but (Cohn excepted) they are soon swept up by the fiesta: their mood is jubilant, they are surrounded by dancers, and they sing, drink and shout with the peasant crowd. Barnes himself is among fellow aficionados; he gains "real emotion" from the bullfights and feels truly elated afterwards. Even his friends seem like "such nice people," though he begins to feel uneasy when an argument breaks out between them. The tension is created by Brett's fiancé, Mike Campbell, who is aware of her numerous infidelities and who seems to accept them with amoral tolerance. Actually he resents them, so that Cohn (the perennial Jewish scapegoat) provides him with a convenient outlet for his feelings. He begins to bait him for following Brett around like a sick steer.

Mike's description is accurate enough. Cohn is always willing to suffer in public and to absorb insults for the sake of true love. On the other hand, he is also "ready to do battle for his lady," and when the chance finally comes, he knocks his rivals down like a genuine knight-errant. With Jake and Mike he has no trouble, but when he charges into Pedro's room to rescue Brett, the results are disastrous: Brett tells him off, the bullfighter refuses to stay knocked down, and no one will shake hands with him at the end, in accord with prep-school custom. When Brett remains with Pedro, Cohn retires to his room, alone and friendless.

This last encounter is the highpoint of the parable, for in the Code

Hero, the Romantic Hero has finally met his match. As the clash between them shows, there is a difference between physical and moral victory, between chivalric stubbornness and real self-respect. Thus Pedro fights to repair an affront to his dignity; though he is badly beaten, his spirit is untouched by his opponent, whereas Cohn's spirit is completely smashed. From the beginning Cohn has based his manhood on skill at boxing, or upon a woman's love, never upon internal strength; but now, when neither skill nor love supports him, he has bludgeoned his way to his own emptiness. Compare his conduct with Romero's, on the following day, as the younger man performs for Brett in the bullring:

> Everything of which he could control the locality he did in front of her all that afternoon. Never once did he look up. . . . Because he did not look up to ask if it pleased he did it all for himself inside, and it strengthened him, and yet he did it for her, too. But he did not do it for her at any loss to himself. He gained by it all through the afternoon.

Thus, where Cohn expends and degrades himself for his beloved, Romero pays tribute without self-loss. His manhood is a thing independent of women, and for this reason he holds special attractions for Jake Barnes.

By now it seems apparent that Cohn and Pedro are extremes for which Barnes is the unhappy medium. His resemblance to Pedro is clear enough: they share the same code, they both believe that a man's dignity depends on his own resources. His resemblance to Cohn is more subtle, but at this stage of the book it becomes grossly evident. Appropriately enough, the exposure comes through the knockout blow from Cohn, which dredges up a strange prewar experience:

> Walking across the square to the hotel everything looked new and changed. . . . I felt as I felt once coming home from an out-of-town football game. I was carrying a suitcase with my football things in it, and I walked up the street from the station in the town I had lived in all my life and it was all new. They were raking the lawns and burning leaves in the road, and I stopped for a long time and watched. It was all strange. Then I went on, and my feet seemed to be a long way off, and everything seemed to come from a long way off, and I could hear my feet walking a great distance

away. I had been kicked in the head early in the game. It was like that crossing the square. It was like that going up the stairs in the hotel. Going up the stairs took a long time, and I had the feeling that I was carrying my suitcase.

Barnes seems to have regressed here to his youthful football days. As he moves on up the stairs to see Cohn, who has been asking for him, he still carries his "phantom suitcase" with him; and when he enters Cohn's room, he even sets it down. Cohn himself has just returned from the fight with Romero: "There he was, face down on the bed, crying. He had on a white polo shirt, the kind he'd worn at Princeton." In other words, Cohn has also regressed to his abject college days: they are both emotional adolescents, about the same age as the nineteen-year-old Romero, who is the only real man among them. Of course, these facts are not spelled out for us, except through the polo shirt and the phantom suitcase, which remind us (inadvertently) of one of those dreamlike fantasies by the Czech genius, Franz Kafka, in which trunks and youthful clothes are symbols of arrested development. Yet there has already been some helpful spelling out in book 1, during a curious (and otherwise pointless) exchange between Cohn and another expatriate, the drunkard Harvey Stone. After first calling Cohn a moron, Harvey asks him to say, without thinking about it, what he would rather do if he could do anything he wanted. Cohn is again urged to say what comes into his head first, and soon replies, "I think I'd rather play football again with what I know about handling myself, now." To which Harvey responds: "I misjudged you. . . . You're not a moron. You're only a case of arrested development."

The first thought to enter Cohn's mind here has been suppressed by Barnes for a long time, but in book 2 the knockout blow releases it: more than anything else, he too would like to "play football again," to prevent that kick to his head from happening, or that smash to the jaw from Cohn, or that sexual wound which explains either blow. For the truth about Barnes seems obvious now: he has always been an emotional adolescent. Like Nick Adams, he has grown up in a society which has little use for manliness; as an expression of that society, the war has robbed him of his dignity as a man and has thus exposed him to indignities with women. We must understand here that the war, the early football game, and the fight with Cohn have this in common: they all involve ugly, senseless, or impersonal forms of violence, in which a man has little chance to set the terms of his own integrity. Hence for Hemingway they represent the kinds of degradation which can occur at any point in modern society—and the violence at Pamplona is our current sample of such degradation. Indeed, the whole confluence of events now points to the social meaning of Jake's wound, for just as Cohn has reduced him to a dazed adolescent, so has Brett reduced him to a slavish pimp. When she asks for his help in her affair with Pedro, Barnes has no integrity to rely on; he can only serve her as Cohn has served her, like a sick romantic steer. Thus, for love's sake, he will allow her to use him as a go-between, to disgrace him with his friend, Montoya, to corrupt Romero, and so strip the whole fiesta of significance. In the next book he will even run to her rescue in Madrid, though by then he can at least recognize his folly and supply his own indictment: "That was it. Send a girl off with one man. Introduce her to another to go off with him. Now go and bring her back. And sign the wire with love. That was it all right." It seems plain, then, that Cohn and Brett have given us a peacetime demonstration, postwar style, of the meaning of Jake's shell wound.

At Pamplona the demonstration continues. Brett strolls through the fiesta with her head high, "as though [it] were being staged in her honor, and she found it pleasant and amusing." When Romero presents her with a bull's ear "cut by popular acclamation," she carries it off to her hotel, stuffs it far back in the drawer of the bed-table, and forgets about it. The ear was taken, however, from the same bull which had killed one of the crowd a few days before, during the dangerous bull-run through the streets; later the entire town attended the man's funeral, along with drinking and dancing societies from nearby communities. For the crowd, the death of this bull was a communal triumph and his ear a token of communal strength; for Brett the ear is a private trophy. In effect, she has robbed the community of its triumph, as she will now rob it of its hero. As an aficionado, Barnes understands this threat too well. These are decadent times in the bullring, marred by false aesthetics; Romero alone has "the old thing," the old "purity of line through the maximum of exposure": his corruption by Brett will complete the decadence. But mainly the young fighter means something more personal to Barnes. In the bullring he combines grace, control and sincerity with manliness; in the fight with Cohn he proves his integrity where skill is lacking. His values are exactly those of the hunter in "Francis Macomber," or of the fisherman in *The Old Man and the Sea*. As one of these few remaining images of independent manhood, he offers Barnes the comfort of vicarious redemption. Brett seems to smash this as she leaves with Pedro for Madrid. To ward off depression, Barnes can only get drunk and retire to bed; the fiesta goes on outside, but it means nothing now: the "good place" has been ruined.

As book 3 begins, Barnes tries to reclaim his dignity and to cleanse himself of the damage at Pamplona. He goes to San Sebastian and sits quietly there in a café, listening to band concerts; or he goes swimming there alone, diving deep in the green waters. Then a telegram from Brett arrives, calling him to Madrid to help her out of trouble. At once he is like Cohn again, ready to serve his lady at the expense of self-respect. Yet in Madrid he learns to accept, emotionally, what he has always faintly understood. As he listens to Brett, he begins to drink heavily, as if her story has driven home a painful lesson. Brett herself feels "rather good" about sending Pedro away: she has at least been able to avoid being "one of these bitches that ruins children." This is a moral triumph for her, as Barnes agrees; but he can scarcely ignore its implications for himself. For when Brett refuses to let her hair grow long for Pedro, it means that her role in life is fixed: she can no longer reclaim her lost womanhood; she can no longer live with a fine man without destroying him. This seems to kill the illusion which is behind Jake's suffering throughout the novel: namely, that if he hadn't been wounded, if he had somehow survived the war with his manhood intact, then he and Brett would have become true lovers. The closing lines confirm his total disillusionment:

> "Oh, Jake," Brett said, "we could have had such a damned good time together."
>
> Ahead was a mounted policeman in khaki directing traffic. He raised his baton. The car slowed suddenly pressing Brett against me.
>
> "Yes," I said, "Isn't it pretty to think so?"

"Pretty" is a romantic word which means here "foolish to consider what could *never* have happened," and not "what can't happen now." The signal for this interpretation comes from the policeman who directs traffic between Brett's speech and Barnes's reply. With his khaki clothes and his preventive baton, he stands for the war and the society which made it, for the force which stops the lovers' car, and which robs them of their normal sexual roles. As Barnes now sees, love itself is dead for their generation. Even without his wound, he would still be unmanly, and Brett unable to let her hair grow long.

Yet according to the opening epigraphs, if one generation is lost and another comes, the earth abides forever; and according to Hemingway himself, the abiding earth is the novel's hero. Perhaps he is wrong on this point, or at least misleading. There are no joyous hymns to the seasons in this novel, no celebrations of fertility and change. The scenic descriptions are accurate enough, but rather flat; there is no deep feeling in them, only fondness, for the author takes less delight in nature than in outdoor sports. He is more concerned, that is, with baiting hooks and catching trout than with the Irati River and more pleased with the grace and skill of the bullfighter than with the bull's magnificence. In fact, it is the bullfighter who seems to abide in the novel, for surely the bulls are dead like the trout before them, having fulfilled their roles as beloved opponents. But Romero is very much alive as the novel ends. When he leaves the hotel in Madrid, he "pays the bill" for his affair with Brett, which means that he has earned all its benefits. He also dominates the final conversation between the lovers, and so dominates the closing section. We learn here that his sexual initiation has been completed and his independence assured. From now on, he can work out his life alone, moving again and again through his passes in the ring, gaining strength, order, and purpose as he meets his own conditions. He provides no literal prescription to follow here, no call to bullfighting as the answer to Barnes's problems; but he does provide an image of integrity, against which Barnes and his generation are weighed and found wanting. In this sense, Pedro is the real hero of the parable, the final moral touchstone, the man whose code gives meaning to a world where love and religion are defunct, where the proofs of manhood are difficult and scarce, and where every man must learn to define his own moral conditions and then live up to them.

Implications of Form in *The Sun Also Rises*

William L. Vance

Part of the achievement of Ernest Hemingway in *The Sun Also Rises* is in the creation of a plot that is both naturalistic and Aristotelian. It suggests the random episodic and circular realism of the former while achieving the dramatic unity and interest of the latter. The philosophical and ethical implications of the compound form are ambiguous, but not, I think, incoherent; they are true to a modern sense of the human situation in a way that implications of the older forms singly are not.

The episodic and circular aspects of the structure, which are the more obvious, are the more commonly observed. There is no beginning and no end; title and epigraph forewarn us to expect no meaning in the form beyond this futile circularity; at the close Jake and Brett ride off into the night whispering vanities like those they whispered chapters and months before and, presumably, like those that, by easy but redundant extension of the book, they could be whispering chapters and years later on. Nothing has happened. Nothing except essentially repetitive episodes of life: drinking and bullfight watching for all, sex for some, and fishing for the rest. And talk and self-torture. There is no conscious human ordering of these events; they occur according to inner impulses, outer stimuli, and the season. Compulsion and reaction are all; and God, if he exists, does not show his hand in the matter. Seen thus in its naturalistic shape, the book's unity would seem to depend on character, symbol, and theme.

From *The Twenties, Poetry and Prose: Twenty Critical Essays,* edited by Richard E. Langford and William E. Taylor. © 1966 by Everett Edwards Press, Inc.

But its unity is nevertheless predominantly a unity of action. In this it is Aristotelian, and from this the book gains a cumulative dramatic interest which stems, as it must, from characters in action, in successive encounters and altering relationships with each other. In the previous view, one might begin at any point on a circle and travel around it as long or as short a distance as necessary to show the random, nonsequential character of the whole. But the starting point of *The Sun Also Rises* is not random; which is to say the book has a beginning. It also has a middle and an end. The action comprises one complete and coherent round, and thus raises questions of meaning that a really discontinuous episodic form, with an arbitrary concluding point, could not.

The action begins with Robert Cohn. The symbolically impotent and necessarily static love affair between Jake Barnes and Lady Brett Ashley exists as a constant, having begun long before the novel opens, and continuing throughout the book and beyond its ending. They try not to see each other, and when they do, they try not to talk about it. Brett is going to marry "this drunkard," Mike Campbell— perhaps; the outcome of that relationship is as uncertain at the end as at the beginning. Jake finds some pleasure in Parisian life, which cannot, however, compensate for his frustrated love for Brett, and which at least once takes the perverted form of picking up a *poule* to whom he must confess his "sickness," and who observes, "Everybody's sick. I'm sick, too." Whatever games they play, everybody's miserable at bottom. That is constant. But this time the particular shape the misery takes is the shape of Robert Cohn, and what he does.

His importance is emphasized by Hemingway—or by Jake (in most questions of the shaping of the narrative, they are interchangeable)— by the long exposition of his character and background in chapter 1. Of the three main characters, he is the only one so treated; expositions of Brett and Jake are absorbed within the narrative and are rendered more dramatically. If it were not for Robert's importance as the active agent in the plot, this primary and stylistically unique exposition would seem disproportionately long, and superfluous in detail. We learn more of his family background, education, and efforts at career and marriage than we ever learn of Brett, and more than there is, evidently, to learn of Jake. Moreover, Robert's organic connection with a psychologically continuous past is pointed up by the distinctive expository method, which would have been inappropriate to characters like Brett and Jake whose lives have been severed, who live in and from the present only, that is, episodically.

The second chapter is more "scenic" (in Henry James's sense) than the first, but it only emphasizes through Robert's immediate presence and direct statement his frustrations and romantic illusions, the underlying motivations causing him to lend a sequential character to the events that follow. The ensuing episodes themselves—or others virtually like them—would have occurred without Cohn, with only that inherent meaning previously described; but what gives them in addition a meaningful sequence and unity is the action of Robert Cohn.

He falls in love with Brett, and goes with her to San Sebastian. To Brett herself and to the others this constitutes an episode only, with no necessary antecedent or consequence; but to Robert it is a beginning: it must mean something and lead somewhere. It must mean love and happiness and children. A naturalistic plot is "like life" in just the way Brett and Jake see life; but Robert sees life in another way. That he expects life to have meaning and sequence and consequence is a part of his gaucherie, but it is this contrary view that Jake and Hemingway superimpose on the naturalistic *tranches de vie* to give their narrative form.

The impression of Cohn given in the first two chapters is unsympathetic, and the precipitate manner in which he falls in love in the third chapter is rendered satirically ("He looked a great deal as his compatriot must have looked when he saw the promised land.") In chapter 5, while questioning Jake about Brett, he appears ridiculous in his idealizing of her: to him, she must be not only "remarkably attractive," which she is to everyone, but also "absolutely fine and straight," a woman of "quality" and "breeding" who wouldn't "marry anybody she didn't love" even though Jake says "She's done it twice." In other words, she is the kind of woman he, Robert Cohn, *deserves*, in consequence of his lovable character (gazing at Brett earlier, "he had a look of eager, deserving expectation"; she is "promised" him as Israel was Moses).

This person is to be the principal agent of the significant action of the book, and concern by the narrator that he may not be taken seriously enough becomes evident. In chapter 6, and despite the already comparatively extensive characterization given him, Jake must say: "Somehow I feel I have not shown Robert Cohn clearly." And he attempts to make him less unsympathetic, attributing to him in fact a "nice, boyish sort of cheerfulness" and normalcy that make him rather more attractive than the cynical sophisticates who reject him. His view of life is at least worth considering as an option to theirs.

The rest of book 1 is devoted to the rendering of the quality of the lives of the others, and to a nasty public scene between Robert and Frances, his mistress to whom (characteristically) he feels an "obligation" and who, partly by this very scene, drives him free. Book 1 concludes, and the action definitely begins, with Robert's going away with Brett. Again, to her this is to be an episode. To Jake she says, "I'm going away from you, and then Michael's coming back." That is all. There is no thought that the antecedent "going away" from Jake and with Robert will at all alter the fact or character of Michael's "coming back"—possibly to marry her.

And so it develops, at least as far as Brett is concerned. In book 2 she comes back, Michael comes back, and perhaps they are going to get married. The stay at San Sebastian should make no difference to any of the three men. To Michael, it doesn't, until later it has consequences: for the reason it doesn't matter is that it should have none. But, Brett is surprised to discover, it does offend Jake when he finds out. Openly sarcastic to her ("Congratulations," he says), his feelings are characteristically mixed:

> I was blind, unforgivingly jealous of what had happened to him. The fact that I took it as a matter of course did not alter that any. I certainly did hate him.

But the greatest difference it makes is, of course, to Robert himself. He, Jake, and Bill Gorton have planned a fishing trip to Spain, to be followed by the fiesta at Pamplona. Brett and Mike ask to be included, but it occurs to her that the situation might be "rough" on Robert Cohn, since she would be with Mike. It is something that she should realize this much; but when Cohn is informed that she and Mike will be going along, his being "keen about it" strikes her and Jake as "rather odd." "He's wonderful," they say.

To Robert Cohn, Brett's joining him (for so he sees it) on the trip to Spain is just what rightly follows from their beginning at San Sebastian. This is a development in their love affair. He writes to her suggesting that he meet her in San Sebastian again, on the way to Spain. But getting no answer, he awaits her—shaved, shampooed, and nervous—in Pamplona. She doesn't arrive. Fearing a misunderstanding, he now feels he must forego the fishing episode altogether—it cannot mean anything in itself to him as it does to Jake and Bill—in order to meet Brett when she does arrive, acting according to the romantic principle that gives continuity to his acts.

In the plot of the novel, the eleventh and twelfth chapters—the fishing episode—exist in a truly episodic fashion, that is, as an interlude which by its very inclusion points up the meaningful sequence of the action linking the other "episodes" and depending upon Robert Cohn for its progression. His very absence from this one is what to a considerable degree gives it its distinctive character. It makes the case, in itself and without Cohn there as a whipping-boy from the opposition, for the impotent Jake's necessarily episodic view of life, in showing that it is not valueless. Some episodes in life, evidently, can be of such character, in their identification with the earth that "abideth forever"—the earth that itself has no beginning, middle, or end—that a sense of sequence and development within the span of an individual life becomes inessential. It shows too, that the absence of sequence need not reduce every episode to the same level of futility: the circle is drawn over hills and valleys, not on a plateau.

The interlude ends, and the action resumes, with telegrams from Brett and from Robert which lead to a regrouping in Pamplona. Comically and naively, Robert is playing the escort to Brett and Mike:

> "I brought them up here," Cohn said.
> "What rot," Brett said. "We'd have gotten here earlier if you hadn't come."
> "You'd never have gotten here."
> "What rot! . . ."
> "Did you get good fishing?" Mike asked. "We wanted to join you."
> "It wasn't bad. We missed you."
> "I wanted to come," Cohn said, "but I thought I ought to bring them."
> "You bring us. What rot."

Robert's sense of obligation again. Love and gratitude for past favors evoke it. To Brett this is "rot," and Robert is a nuisance. He persists in being one as the fiesta proceeds, and the person most irritated by this is of course Mike: "Is Robert Cohn going to follow Brett around like a steer all the time?" To Robert he says: "Don't sit there looking like a bloody funeral. What if Brett did sleep with you? She's slept with lots of other people." And to Jake: "Brett's gone off with men. But . . . they didn't come and hang about afterward." To which Brett adds:

"Damned good chaps. . . . Michael and I understand each other." This nonsequential view of life is what Robert cannot understand. Michael becomes belligerent, but a fight is avoided, and later, when he is to meet Robert again, he asks, "How should I meet Cohn?" The answer is: "Just act as though nothing had happened." That is the motto of the episodic world.

But Cohn persists. "He could not stop looking at Brett. It seemed to make him happy. It must have been pleasant for him to see her looking so lovely, and know he had been away with her and that everyone knew it. They could not take that away from him." Jake here attributes to Cohn his own way of seeing things: that an experience can be self-contained and possessed in inviolate separateness forever (in the next chapter he says of a passage in Turgenev: "I would always have it.") But an episode is unsatisfactory to Cohn except as part of a larger whole, and his continuing pursuit of Brett leads to the climax of the book. He follows her and Jake to church, he sits with Brett and Mike at the bullring. He cannot believe there will be no third act wedding climaxing his love affair with Brett. So he is there when Mike, drunken and maddened by Brett's newly developed attraction to the bullfighter Romero, needs a victim. But Mike's attacking *him* seems to imply that he is a rival, that in fact his affair is progressing: "His face had the sallow, yellow look it got when he was insulted, but somehow he seemed to be enjoying it. The childish, drunken heroics of it. It was his affair with a lady of title." Mike challenges him. "He stood waiting, . . . proudly and firmly waiting for the assault, ready to do battle for his lady love." But the chivalric opportunity is lost again. The others maneuver Mike away. All Cohn can do is volunteer to sit with Brett. " 'O, don't!' Brett said. 'For God's sake, go off somewhere.' " And so, obedient, he goes. Brett and Jake agree that he has "behaved very badly" all along, and that "He had a chance to behave so well." This, of course, by their episodic conception of behavior. But Brett does not miss his point of view. She has on a previous occasion obliquely said that love interferes with the values of even episodic people, and now she says, "You know I do know how he feels. He can't believe it didn't mean anything." Seeing him later waiting in the shadow of an arcade, she says, "Poor devil! . . . I hate his damned suffering." But she does not feel responsible, because she refuses to believe that her own behavior implied anything in itself and she certainly intended nothing by it; the fault then, is in him who draws inferences.

It takes more than words to convince Robert Cohn. It takes another action from which, if he drew the same inferences, he could only conclude the error of those he applied to himself. The decisive action is Brett's going off with Romero, motivated both by his attractiveness and her disgust with the behavior of Robert and Mike. Brett's being with Mike has signified nothing to Cohn, since Mike had simply been there first, and Brett could break with him. Cohn's egotism, emphasized from the beginning, prevents him from seeing the truth about Brett from the fact of her going off with him while "engaged" to Mike; that seemed only natural. But Brett's leaving them both for Romero is very clear in its meaning, and in response Robert can only resort to physical violence (also prepared for on the very first page). He beats up Jake, for arranging the assignation, then he beats up Romero, and tries to take Brett away. This finishes him with everyone, and is the climax of his affair with Brett: this is what came of it all. "I'm going away in the morning," he says.

> "I just couldn't stand it about Brett. I've been through hell, Jake. It's been simply hell. When I met her down here Brett treated me as though I were a perfect stranger. I just couldn't stand it. We lived together at San Sebastian."

To him it is incomprehensible. "We lived together at San Sebastian." It seemed such an absolute proof. And then to be treated as a stranger! As though to assure himself that something endures, that something links the episodes together, he tries to patch up his friendship with Jake. "You were the only friend I had, and I loved Brett so. . . . Please forgive me, Jake. . . . You'll shake hands, won't you?" But he says, "Now everything's gone. Everything." So Jake was wrong. They *could* take it away from him. To a man for whom the meaning and beauty of an episode depends upon the way it fits into a romantic whole, the incompletion of the whole nullifies the episode.

By her affair with Romero Brett has rid herself of Robert, and from this point the action falls toward the denouement, that is, it comes full circle. The morning after, Jake observes: "It was the first time I had seen her in the old happy, careless way since before she went off with Cohn." In the brief book 3, there remains only the necessity of Brett's ending her new episode with Romero; she ends it, ironically, because he expects it to lead somewhere: to marriage and children, to be something more than an episode. But Brett knows herself at least this well, to know that the attempt would have been ruinous for Romero. She is now what she is—a woman of episodic character—however much she may believe that with Jake she could have been different. Out of the whole sequence, so strangely linked together by the illusions of Robert Cohn, for Brett there is only one gain: the riddance of that very man. "I'm all right again. He's wiped out that damned Cohn." To which Jake says, "Good." They are back where they started.

Hemingway's superimposing of a pyramidal plot upon a circular and episodic naturalistic one gives his book a greater unity than the latter alone could have provided. At the same time a meaningful thematic emphasis is made by the tension that exists between the two plot forms, because they inherently suggest differing views of life which are in varying degrees held by the characters themselves, as the preceding analysis has shown. The two forms are unified into a third distinct but ambiguous form through the point of view of the narrator. Jake Barnes is of necessity an episodic man (in that his life must lack the integrity of conventional social fulfillment or religious commitment), but his entire interest in telling the story of Robert Cohn—who is, after all, only one out of several lovers of Brett, all of whom he must resent—depends upon Cohn's *not* holding the episodic view. Jake's emotional duplicity is what impressionistically unifies the circular and pyramidal forms. Although Cohn, who in the naiveté of his romantic expectations acts out a pathetic three-part drama of love and loss, is of insufficient stature to sustain his role on a heroic level even in his own eyes, his story is further blunted and rendered absurd by the incongruous naturalistic (anti-romantic) frame of reference, by the unresponsiveness of the other characters, and by the complicated attitude of Jake ("I was . . . jealous . . . I took it as a matter of course.") The pyramid of Cohn's affair can be discerned only through the dead sea waters of Jake's own love for Brett. Although Robert links the separate episodes of this particular round together, in the end they only merge, in effect, into one: the Robert Cohn Episode, to be followed by innumerable others.

The peculiar plot of *The Sun Also Rises* thus avoids an implicit dogmatism of form to be found in abstracted conceptions of traditional forms. The linear episodic plot implies a lack of coherent sequence to events but also implies freedom, variety, and unconditioned potentialities in the experiences of the unifying character, as can be seen from *Moll Flanders* to *Augie March*; it may be modified, as in the middle part of *Huckleberry Finn*, by the recurrence and intensification of a situation

(Huck's alliance with Jim) which stimulates moral growth and discovery in that character; or, through virtual repetition of pattern it may suggest circularity and thus either futility (as, in isolation, this aspect of *Sun* does) or, if united with natural or religious imagery, a positive cyclical recurrence (birth, death, resurrection), as in *My Antonia*. The pyramidal plot affirms meaningful sequence—even necessity—of events *developing* in response to deliberate actions of characters and having an inevitable ethical consequence: the best examples in American literature are probably *The Scarlet Letter* and *The Great Gatsby*. Gatsby and his story have significant points in common with Robert Cohn and his, but are allowed to dominate the book, with the episodic characters and their world subordinated to Gatsby's attempt to fulfill *his* romantic expectations. There is in *Gatsby* also a finer and purer irony in the point of view of the narrator (Nick fortunately does not love his cousin Daisy), so that Gatsby's dream seems beautiful as well as childish, and his fate even more tragic than pathetic and absurd. In comparison with *The Great Gatsby*, which truly (if through irony) affirms the possibility of a romantically integrated life, *The Sun Also Rises* seems more assertive of the naturalistic circle of futile discontinuity, more like Chekov's *Three Sisters*. And so it is; my point is simply that while Robert is used to give unity to a series of happenings which still persists in presenting itself as episodic and circular and futile (partly because, as opposed to Gatsby's case, Robert's failure nullifies his whole attempt, and partly because the episodes are given at least equal development in their own discontinuous character), nevertheless the mere existence within the book of a conception of sequence, and its artistic exploitation throughout, in effect present it as an option.

One might argue that the manner in which it is presented, with Robert Cohn as its representative and his puling end as its outcome, renders it rather emphatically *not* as a "live" option, and perhaps even goes further toward negating it than its absolute exclusion would have done. My answer to this is that the assumptions Cohn represents can survive a bad representative of them and his particular fate. Such an assumption, for instance, as that one person acting in relation to another is responsible to a degree for the inferences the other draws from his acts. If one can say that Cohn ought not to have concluded anything from Brett's sleeping with him, one can also say that Brett ought to have discovered beforehand what kind of conclusions Cohn was likely to draw from her sleeping with him; but the egotism of the self-consciously sophisticated (like Daisy: "God, I'm sophisticated!";

and Brett: "We've all been around.") allows them to believe that anyone not equally so can suffer the consequences of associating with them ("I hate his damned suffering"). Romantic ethical idealism is at the heart of Hemingway's work: it is the loss of that idealism which is regretted, and it is there to be contemplated by the reader even if it is rendered in terms of characters who as a result of their several wounds have abjured it as inefficacious, or through those like Robert whose particular attempts to act by it fail. The cynicism, bitterness, and self-pity of the point of view of those who have given up hardly recommend it to the reader either, even if he acknowledges it as more "realistic" and as having compensations in the practice of the "code" and in the self-contained sensual pleasures of Paris and Spain. Whatever truth and viability there is in the point of view of the episodic characters would have been more assertive if Robert Cohn had not been there to present—however feebly—a challenge to their position and to evoke the streaks of meanness and false superiority in Jake and Brett.

Further comparisons emphasize this point. The experiences of Augie March are just as discontinuous but contain an element of joy wholly absent from *The Sun Also Rises*, and thus represent the episodic option more attractively, just as Gatsby shows the other view in its more beautiful if still naive potentials. But if Augie suggests an episodic life more joyous and hopeful, we can see that naturalistic plots can also be made more assertive of pessimism and despair. The design of *Sister Carrie*, for instance: here again is a book in which clear, unifying lines of development are submerged within an episodic world. It is made to *seem* to have the random quality of life itself, as *Sun* is, but the lines of development hidden in it, in contrast, themselves demonstrate a thesis about the "vagaries of fortune." Carrie rises, Hurstwood declines, and Drouet swaggers through on an even level; and not from any moral causes or free choices, but because of incomprehensible forces of determinism. Or consider Frank Norris's *McTeague* (weak as it is, probably our purest example of the *roman experimental*, where all is tightly sequential but deterministic): take this beast with latent capacities for sex and violence, put him in this environment, add one tiny blonde female (who herself is thus subjected to experiment), add one quantity of gold, take away a dental license, and see what happens. This "experiment" is carried out in part through "episodes" of great verisimilitude, each of which contributes to the general realism while playing its part in the dogmatic design by providing behavioristic evidence of environmental and physiological forces.

In contrast to any of the other novels I have mentioned, how tentative and even regretful of its implications, how unassertive for all its clarity, seems the unique form of *The Sun Also Rises*. It attains its high degree of artistic unity, and yet remains true to the essential fragmenting skepticism of its time and of its author, to their distrust of absolutes. A nonsequential style handled thus is not asserting non sequitur as final truth, or a dogmatic agnosticism like Dreiser's. It rather tells only what it sees, while suggesting what romantic arteries of continuity it *wishes* might be shown to exist. ("Isn't it pretty to think so?")

Ernest Hemingway
and the Rhetoric of Escape

Robert O. Stephens

When in *The Sun Also Rises* Hemingway depicts the American writer Bill Gorton telling Jake Barnes what their homeland thinks of a newspaperman who refuses to return home, he presents a scene epitomizing a key movement in twentieth-century literature: "You're an expatriate. You've lost touch with the soil. You get precious. Fake European standards have ruined you. You drink yourself to death. You become obsessed by sex. You are an expatriate, see? You hang around cafes." Like these two men, Hemingway's protagonists from first to last serve as prime commentators on the tendency of the spiritually dislocated of the age to seek their salvation by escaping from the horrors of the age. In this essay I should like to explore the responses of Hemingway's people to their times, particularly as they are depicted in his uniquely suitable idiom. This escape motif appears in virtually all Hemingway's stories and novels. The most intense presentation, however, appears in those works of the twenties and early thirties—*In Our Time* (1925), *The Sun Also Rises* (1926), *Men without Women* (1927), *A Farewell to Arms* (1929), and *Winner Take Nothing* (1933).

All these narratives show that escape means more than alienation of the artist from his homeland. It is a significant contribution of Hemingway to world literature that he has explored the possibilities and implications of escape more than has any other writer, including

From *The Twenties, Poetry and Prose: Twenty Critical Essays,* edited by Richard E. Langford and William E. Taylor. © 1966 by Everett Edwards Press, Inc.

Henry James. Because of his explorations we can get a clear rationale of escape that is true for his time and for all times the literary tradition speaks for. As a narrative motif, escape quickly identifies the issues of the conflict. It is one of three possible responses to an intolerable situation, the other two being resignation and struggle to change the predicament. Protagonists choose escape when the menace of the world seems too great and the stature of man too small to challenge the order of things and when man is still too rebellious or too horrified to accept things as they are. Such was the predicament of the apocalypse-minded Christians of the first century, such was the mind of the Leatherstockings and Huckleberry Finns of nineteenth-century American literature, and such is the mind of Hemingway's heroes of the twentieth century.

Implicit also in this response is the pattern the escapist must follow through the three stages of rejection, avoidance, and quest for new values or a new situation. This process emphasizes directly perceived experience rather than abstract teachings about experience. The protagonist is an agent of action rather than speculation. He rejects the initial situation because it is too menacing to his body or his pride. He escapes *from* that situation by acts of avoidance—physical flight or emotional withdrawal. He escapes *to* another situation to find more tolerable experience. Escape must thus be understood as a technique or process, not an end in itself.

Hemingway's people live in a pragmatic world where independently existing values no longer prevail. Their values are tied to actions, to the deeds themselves which are moral or immoral, not to any outside ethical frame of reference. Thus Jake Barnes describes his relationship to the world: "Perhaps as you went along you did learn something. I did not care what it was all about. All I wanted to know was how to live in it. Maybe if you found out how to live in it you learned from that what it was all about." The exiles' research in the vanities, then, as Robert Penn Warren notes (*Kenyon Review*, 1947), is not a random sampling of sensations but a disciplined quest for pragmatic values derived from the basic, sensational level of perception. Having recognized the invalidity of irrelevance of abstract traditional values, as Frederic Henry does in *A Farewell to Arms*, they occupy themselves with concrete details of moment-to-moment living. Their future they make sensation by sensation, syllable by syllable.

In *The Sun Also Rises*, which I should like to use as the focal point of my examination, one of the key distinctions in characters is that between the truly questing escapist and the pseudo-expatriate. The true expatriates, or the insiders of the escape experience, are self-directed; they share a common experience that they recognize without speaking about it. They are in rebellion against the values of their homelands and live in Paris to be free of conventions that hamper their quests. Their belief in the validity of the immediate and individual action frees them of claims by the outside world. They form a minority society always in flux. Wherever their individual quests take them, they deny the previous experience or locale by occupying themselves with only the present action. Thus Brett Ashley takes a succession of lovers in her quest for the one who can give back to her a sense of spiritual integrity she has lost. Similarly the insider savors the individual drink, the individual meal, the individual scene as the basis of value. Jake Barnes notes this about Count Mippipopolous when he says of the dinner he shares in the Bois with Brett and the Count: "It was a good dinner. Food had an excellent place in the count's values. So did wine. The count was in fine form during the meal. So was Brett. It was a good party."

Another criterion of the insiders is their awareness of *nada*, the knowledge that not only social values but also personal beliefs in one's immortality—emotional beliefs, not just abstract recognition of the fact of death—have been seriously damaged by the war. Jake has his nighttime terrors when he must keep a light on to ward off the irrational fears of darkness associated with his wounding. Brett's actions reflect her inner torture, which Jake notes when he says, "She was afraid of so many things." Count Mippipopolous qualifies through his participation in seven wars and four revolutions, during which he has received his illusion-destroying arrow wounds. Bill Gorton admits he is "daunted" sometimes, and Harvey Stone knows horrors that make him hide in his room "like a cat." The outsiders are those like Robert Cohn, Mrs. Braddocks, Robert Prentiss, the artist Zizi, the bal musette homosexuals, and the Paris and Pamplona tourists who are unhaunted by *nada*, have no real cause for rebellion against their societies, and are messy and undisciplined as they imitate without comprehension the actions of the insiders.

These intellectual and emotional wounds are the basis of the expatriates' rhetoric. Part of their code is that they must not talk directly about their knowledge of *nada*, though it is implied in every word. Robert Cohn's failure to observe this causes the others to scorn his "damned suffering" when his illusions are shattered at Pamplona. This is what Brett means when she tells Jake, after renouncing the young matador Romero, "Don't let's ever talk about it. Please don't let's ever talk about it." But there are ways they talk about their predicament indirectly. By extremely simple language loaded with hidden connotations, by various ironies, by personal symbols, and by allusions, they carry on the business of their quest. It is presumably the only language they can use and still be true to the exigencies of their search.

Both Jake Barnes and Count Mippipopolous comment on the ostensibly simple rhetoric of the insiders. Jake links Brett's language with the ultra-simple, sensuous, and even primitive language of the Eskimo or the Cherokee:

> What rot, I could hear Brett say it. What rot! When you were with English you got into the habit of using English expressions in your thinking. The English spoken language— the upper classes anyway—must have fewer words than the Eskimo. Of course I didn't know anything about the Eskimo. Maybe Eskimo was a fine language. Say the Cherokee. I didn't know anything about Cherokee either. The English talked with inflected phrases. One phrase to mean everything. I liked them, though. I like the way they talked.

It is this implied relationship between speaker and listener that carries the inflected meaning past the simple word and elliptical syntax. The count also notes that much remains unstated in Brett's talk. When he complains that she never finishes her sentences, she points out that she leaves them for the listener to finish as he likes. The count calls it "a very interesting system." As to those shorthand words *fine, nice,* and *grand,* Harry Levin in his study of Hemingway's style (*Kenyon Review*, 1951) shows that the fictional characters use the terms as agreed-upon counters of evaluation, not attempts at description.

Jake Barnes finds the simple language adequate to convey the immediacy of his sensuous perceptions. At San Sebastian after his upsetting experiences at the Pamplona fiesta, he goes through a series of simplified, ritualistic actions to regain control of his feelings. These actions constitute a series of individual perceptions linked by the arbitrary control of a mind that chooses to see and feel these sensations as the calming ones he needs. Concrete, separate, monosyllabic, the statements are close to the elemental language he noted in Brett; now they combine description with evaluation:

After lunch I went up to my room, read a while, and went to sleep. When I woke, it was half past four. I found my swimming suit, wrapped it with a comb in a towel, and went downstairs and walked up the street to the Concha. The tide was about halfway out. The beach was smooth and firm, and the sand yellow. I went to a bathing-cabin, undressed, put on my suit, and walked across the smooth sand to the sea. The sand was warm under bare feet. There were quite a few people in the water and on the beach. . . . I waded out. The water was cold. As a roller came I dove, swam out under water, and came to the surface with all the chill gone. I swam out to the raft, pulled myself up, and lay on the planks.

Irony is a second device used by the expatriates to say more by saying less. Not only does irony reflect their distrust of language, it also serves as an index to their awareness of a contradictory and chaotic world. This mode of perception and statement appears particularly in the incongruous dinner between the emasculated Jake and the prostitute Georgette. As Jake inwardly mocks himself for his act, he notes without comment the discrepancies of their predicament. His summary of their dinner conversation is all terse understatement: "We would probably have gone on and discussed the war and agreed it was in reality a calamity for civilization, and perhaps would have been better avoided." Similarly, the English fisherman Wilson-Harris hints by understatement at his knowledge of *nada* and his authority for belonging to the insiders: "I've not had much fun since the war." Jake uses even more effectively the ironic pause of the enthymeme or truncated syllogism to indicate his disappointment at the dinner with Georgette: "She grinned and I saw why she made a point of not laughing. With her mouth closed she was a rather pretty girl." But perhaps the most sustained use of irony occurs in the talks between Jake and Bill at the Burguete inn and during their fishing trip to the Irati. At those times Bill Gorton, a fully initiated though temporary expatriate, reminds Jake that "Irony and Pity" are the watchwords of the insiders.

A third way the escapists say something without saying it overtly is to attach private and special meanings to ordinary words. That this manner of statement has its beginnings in their way of feeling can be seen in the passage of Jake's narration after Brett misses their meeting at the Crillon. Riding in a taxi to the Dome café, he notes: "The Boulevard Raspail always made dull riding. It was like a certain stretch on the P.L.M. between Fontainebleau and Montereau that always made me feel bored and dead and dull until it was over. I suppose it is some association of ideas that makes those dead places in a journey." This is the mind also of Frederic Henry in *A Farewell to Arms* when he confesses a special affection for the name "Archbishop Ireland" because it reminds him of "island" and escape from the war. In *The Sun Also Rises* the expatriates make a special meaning for the word "steer" after they see the unloading of the bulls at Pamplona and Mike Campbell goads Robert Cohn with the term: "I would have thought you'd love being a steer, Robert . . . They lead such a quiet life. They never say anything and they're always hanging around so." Jake and Bill see much meaning for the word "utilize" in their talk at the Irati. For them it signifies their quest for pragmatic and sensuous values, and they use it to mark the significance of their eating and drinking: "Let us utilize the fowls of the air. Let us utilize the product of the vine. Will you utilize a little, brother?" They pass the term on to Wilson-Harris, and Jake notes that by the time to return to Pamplona, the Englishman certifies his initiation by using the term.

Perhaps the key device of the escapists' rhetoric is allusion. Because of their knowledge of something too obscene to say openly, they speak obliquely. They say a name and imply the qualities that go with the name, or mention an attribute and suggest the unspeakable name. Allusion is the key to the code language of the expatriates. During their "Irony and Pity" talk at Burguete, Bill tells Jake the degree of the insiders' acceptance of the phrase by saying "It's just like the Fratellinis used to be." Thus Jake understands the acridly comic possibilities of the phrase by Bill's mention of the cabaret clown act. The conversations at the inn and at the fishing stream are filled with such allusions— hints of the Freudian-Krafft-Ebing fad and mockery of Kipling's psychological innocence ("The Colonel's Lady and Judy O'Grady are Lesbians under their skin"), the Dayton evolution trial and Bryan's fundamentalism ("I reverse the order. For Bryan's sake. As a tribute to the Great Commoner. First the chicken; then the egg"), and the prohibition-Catholic dispute ("I went to Notre Dame with Wayne B. Wheeler"). Some of the allusions reflect the most personal preoccupations of the speakers. Bill speaks analogously of Henry James's rumored sexual injury to speak of Jake's when he says: "That's the sort of thing that can't be spoken of. That's what you ought to work up into a mystery. Like Henry's bicycle."

Allusion works still another way through Jake's narration. He involves the readers as an insider to the extent that he cites actions and scenes familiar to the initiated and implies the reader's understanding, as though he were across the table at the Select. When he describes the walk he and Bill take back from Madame Lecomte's restaurant, he mentions the landmarks they pass as though they are totally familiar and need only to be mentioned to be evoked. "We crossed the bridge and walked up the Rue du Cardinal Lemoine. It was steep walking, and we went all the way to the Place Contrescarpe." He links allusion with the quest for sensate values and implies a common understanding about the qualities of specific drinks. He records ordering and drinking his Jack Rose, his Anis del Mono, or his *vieux marc* without apparent need of characterizing it.

Hemingway's rhetoric of escape has, however, another major manifestation besides that of the language of the insiders. Like the expatriates, Hemingway the novelist must find a proper idiom for his theme. He finds it in the pattern of escape, which serves as a structural guide for all levels of his novel. The pattern of rejection, avoidance, and quest is a repeated one when seen along the whole range of Hemingway's writing. Numerous critics have noted that the novelist's heroes embody a continuum of experience, so that later heroes incorporate the experience of earlier ones. Colonel Robert Cantwell of *Across the River and into the Trees* (1950) most clearly exemplifies this pattern. At fifty, he has lived through his initiation by wounding as have Nick Adams and Frederic Henry, sampled the expatriate life known to Jake Barnes, and witnessed the loss of Spain as has Robert Jordan. What is also noticeable about these protagonists is that each carries out a cycle of the escape pattern and in his quest for new values goes on to another predicament which he rejects and avoids in order to turn to another situation and enter another cycle. This pattern represents the process of learning for the cumulative hero. Nick Adams rejects provincial Michigan to escape to war, but in war he experiences further horror and escapes to make his separate peace. Frederic Henry carries out the latter part of that pattern with more emphatic feelings. Jake Barnes begins where Nick Adams and Frederic Henry leave off, and he, at first turning to the expatriate life, finds it discredited at the chaotic fiesta of Pamplona, then turns to the ever smaller society of aficionados. This cycle is then followed through by Hemingway himself as narrator in *Death in the Afternoon*. And the pattern goes on through all the protagonists' careers.

Seen as an abstract design this pattern suggests a traveling circle— philosophically a vicious circle if one fails to note the development from one protagonist to another. This tendency is at least one of the reasons for the critical labeling of Hemingway as a writer of despair. This circular design can also be seen as the aesthetic plan in each work. Particularly does it describe *The Sun Also Rises*. When Jake Barnes rides with Lady Brett in the Madrileño taxi in book 3, he is ostensibly back where he started— riding stoically with Brett in the Parisian taxi of book 1. He has, however, outgrown his bohemian friends and is emotionally ready to seek the values of the matador Romero, the only one in the book who overtly escapes the futility of the expatriate circle.

That this circular design serves as the rhetorical basis of Hemingway's statement can be seen on several levels of organization in the book. The epigraph to the novel suggests that although one generation considers itself uniquely lost, it is part of a succession of generations on the earth: "The sun also riseth, and the sun goeth down, and hasteth to the place where he arose . . . The wind goeth toward the south, and turneth about unto the north; it whirleth about continually, and the wind returneth again according to his circuits."

On the paragraph level this pattern prevails. The Hemingway paragraph, particularly when Jake Barnes rises to comment through narration on the theme, is the well-rounded paragraph with the final sentence that turns back on the rest of the paragraph. The comment at the beginning of the Pamplona festival serves as an example:

> The fiesta was really started. It kept up day and night for seven days. The dancing kept up, the drinking kept up, the noise went on. The things that happened could only have happened during a fiesta. Everything became quite unreal finally and it seemed as though nothing could have any consequences. It seemed out of place to think of consequences during the fiesta. All during the fiesta you had the feeling, even when it was quiet, that you had to shout any remark to make it heard. It was the same feeling about any action. It was a fiesta and it went on for seven days.

This paragraph style derives from Hemingway's apprentice period when the total composition was paragraph length. The sketches of *In*

Our Time all gain their ironic, deadpan forcefulness by this device. Chapter 3, for example, foreshadows the pattern in the novel:

> We were in a garden at Mons. Young Buckley came in with his patrol from across the river. The first German I saw climbed up over the garden wall. We waited till he got one leg over and then potted him. He had so much equipment on and looked awfully surprised and fell down into the garden. Then three more came over further down the wall. We shot them. They all came just like that.

And so do the paragraphs.

The relationship between the sentences of the paragraph and the circular design is best seen in the device of accretion through repetition. As F. J. Hoffman points out in his study *The Twenties*, Hemingway's prose gives evidence of his having observed Gertrude Stein's rule to maintain a continuum of perception by "beginning again and again" and by using all the perceptions that convey immediacy. Thus the almost arbitrary separateness of each sentence as a perception is at least partially counterbalanced by the aesthetic progress through accretion of ideas and perceptions. During one of Jake's nighttime terrors the subject and manner of the moment-by-moment sequence are integrated through the traveling circle sentence. Key words like *thinking* and *jumping* recur in a kind of incremental repetition to suggest both continuity and "beginning again and again":

> I lay awake thinking and my mind jumping around. Then I couldn't keep away from it, and I started to think about Brett and all the rest of it went away. I was thinking about Brett and my mind started jumping around and started to go on in sort of smooth waves. Then all of a sudden I started to cry. Then after a while it was better and I lay in bed and listened to the heavy trams go by and way down the street, and then I went to sleep.

Here the continuity is aided by overt connectives. In the fiesta paragraph earlier the continuity is achieved with only implied connectives. In both cases the circulate design haunts the passage.

In both act and idiom Hemingway thus clarifies the escapist mind of his twentieth-century heroes and readers. In *Exile's Return* Malcolm Cowley, himself an expatriate as well as chronicler of the times, attests to the degree of truth that the "lost generation" found in Hemingway's novel: "young men tried to get as imperturbably drunk as the hero, young women of good families took a succession of lovers in the same heartbroken fashion as the heroine, they all talked like Hemingway characters and the name was fixed." Perhaps the greatest achievement of Hemingway's rhetoric of escape then was to make all his readers potentially insiders to the great dark secret.

Meyer Wolfsheim and Robert Cohn: A Study of a Jewish Type and Stereotype

Josephine Z. Knopf

For centuries the Jew has been an important literary figure, especially in the literature of the West. He has embodied a convenient mythology which has often proved indispensable to the writer of imaginative fiction. This mythology has taken many shapes: the Jews as villain, the Jew as degenerate, the Jew as wanderer, the Jew as parasite to mention but a few. In modern times, and especially since the devastating experience of World War II, the literary role of the Jew has increasingly become a dual one. On the one hand he maintains something of his ancient, mysterious, and somewhat impalatable flavor, while on the other he merges as an heroic figure, long-suffering and imbued with the wisdom of the ages. In fact, he has become freed of the ancient onus to the extent that it has been possible in this century for Jewish figures to appear to the serious reading public in a variety not previously possible. Consider Proust, Joyce, and Kafka, for example.

It is not at all surprising that such extensive use of Jewish characters in literature would result, on occasion, in their misuse. It is the purpose here to examine two such occasions: Meyer Wolfsheim in *The Great Gatsby* and Robert Cohn in *The Sun Also Rises*, to show that Meyer Wolfsheim can best be understood as a "villainous Jew" and Robert Cohn as a "shlemiel," and that as Jewish figures both are inauthentic and unrealistic failures. The terms "villainous Jew" and "shlemiel" are perhaps widely, but certainly not universally, under-

From *Tradition: A Journal of Orthodox Jewish Thought* 10, no. 3 (Spring 1969). © 1969 by the Rabbinical Council of America.

stood. Thus, a short discussion of both will be given in order to avoid possible misunderstanding.

Although neither Wolfsheim nor Cohn is a protagonist each serves as an interesting example, for each plays an important role in the work in which he appears, and, perhaps more to the point, the Jewishness of each dominates his characterization despite the fact that such a characterization is not really demanded by the text in question. In each case the Jewishness appears to be superimposed upon the text, perhaps as a reflection of some private attitude held by the author (or perhaps the author's response to what he feels to be a *widespread* attitude among his reading public).

It is, in fact, well known that in the 1920s, some of the literary *avant garde* (among them Hemingway and Fitzgerald) revealed anti-Semitic attitudes, both in their essays in their imaginative writing: here the Jew very often appeared as a representative of the modern bourgeoisie which these writers attacked without mercy. As an example of this, Fitzgerald in "Echoes of the Jazz Age" writes: "by 1928 Paris had grown suffocating. With each new shipment of Americans spewed up by the boom the quality fell off, until toward the end there was something sinister about the crazy boat loads . . . I remember a fat Jewess, inlaid with diamonds, who sat behind us at the Russian Ballet and said as the curtain rose, "Thad's luffly, dey ought to baint a picture of it' . . . it was evident that money and power were falling into the hands of people in comparison with whom the leader of a village Soviet would be a gold-mine of judgment and culture."

Where Hemingway is concerned we cannot avoid considering the anti-Semitic comments that run through *The Sun Also Rises*. It is interesting to note that various remarks about Robert Cohn's Jewishness (appearing in the Modern Library edition on pages 98, 104, 148, 168, 170, 184, 211, 214, 218) which the editors apparently considered to be anti-Semitic were deleted from the first Bantam edition of the book, without the knowledge of either the author or his regular publisher, Scribner's. Hemingway, upon having this brought to his attention denied the possibility: "If you think the book is anti-Semitic you must be out of your mind or at least not in full possession of your faculties." It would be incorrect and unfair to Hemingway to assert that the book is an anti-Semitic tract; certainly anti-Semitism is not its intention. However, there are characters in the novel who do express anti-Semitic feelings, and their remarks most certainly color our perception of Cohn, so that we see in him few redeeming qualities.

The situation of Meyer Wolfsheim is different, but with some of the same overtones. In *The Great Gatsby*, there is a scene in which Wolfsheim is the man that is said to have "fixed" the World Series in 1919. The fact "staggers" Nick, for it had never occurred to him that "one man could start to play with the faith of fifty million people with the singlemindedness of a burglar blowing up a safe." It is this luncheon scene which elicited the admiration of Edith Wharton in her congratulatory letter to Fitzgerald on the publication of his book. "The lunch with Hildesheim, [the name was changed to Wolfsheim in the subsequent edition of the book] and his every appearance afterward, make me auger still greater things." And in another part of the letter, "meanwhile, it's enough to make this reader happy to have met your perfect Jew."

Of the several Jewish stereotypes in Western literature that of the "villainous Jew" seems to predominate. A Jewish type of great importance in Yiddish and Hebrew literature is that of the "shlemiel." Between these two there is an important distinction to be drawn, and it is advisedly that we have referred to one as a "stereotype" and to the other as a "type." The villainous Jew of literature is a synthesis of various elements drawn from many individual Jews; he is essentially a receptacle for a large number of evil characteristics that could, at one time or another, be attributed to individual Jews. The "villainous Jew" thus remains a lifeless, stereotyped outgrowth of the antipathy felt toward Jews by the world at large. The "shlemiel," on the other hand, is a genuine Jewish figure, dating back to biblical times at least. His appearance in literature is rooted in conditions existing in the Jewish community. It can be observed that in the shlemiel's first appearance in literature most of his basic characteristics are already in evidence, that in contradistinction to the villainous Jew he did not emerge as a composite of characteristics pieced together so as to form a convenient stereotype, but rather he developed organically as a necessary response to a real environment.

Endowing a character with a Jewish name and referring to him as a Jew, a writer does not automatically create an authentic Jew, that is, a character who would have to be essentially different if he were not Jewish. Fitzgerald in Wolfsheim and Hemingway in Cohn have not done so. Curiously, the failure of Wolfsheim to be an authentic Jewish character must be explained on grounds that are not merely different from those given to explain Cohn's failure, but in fact, on diametrically opposed, even contradictory grounds. Wolfsheim fails because he fulfills the role of the villainous Jew too faithfully; Cohn because he does not fulfill the role of the schlemiel faithfully enough. In light of the discussion of the villainous Jew and the schlemiel given earlier this is not the paradox it might otherwise appear to be.

The myth of the Jew as villain as well as his description can be found in the biblical story of Herod where much of that description is recalled in the character of Shylock, which by the Renaissance became an accepted caricature of the Jew.

By the nineteenth century things could be predicted about the Jew, and it is here that we come very close to Wolfsheim. The stereotype of the Jew was that of a "fairly thoroughgoing materialist, a physical coward, an opportunist in money matters, a bit of a wizard in peddling his pharmaceutica; . . . secretive in his living habits, servile in his relations with Christians, whom he abominated. For physical sign-posts he had an outlandish nose, an unpleasant odor, and frequently a speech impediment also. He was a literalist and stickler in debate and a trained Talmudist in his logic . . . His conversation was attended by much frenzied gesticulating . . . He himself sat spider-like, in the center of an impressive commercial network. Other animal metaphors which described him were the hog, the dog, the rat, the vulture, the weasel, the fox, the toad, the serpent, and the wasp. As an ageless creature less sinned against than sinning, he hardly qualified for tragedy; on the other hand, his repulsive physiognomy, his eccentric habits, and his hostile motives conspired to suit him ideally for the purposes of the comic and the horrific." (Edgar Rosenberg, *From Shylock To Svengali: Jewish Stereotypes in English Fiction*).

In *The Great Gatsby*, we first meet Wolfsheim at his luncheon appointment with Jay Gatsby and Nick Carraway. Here we are told that Wolfsheim is a "flat-nosed Jew." The fact that he is Jewish seems to play no role either at this point or in the rest of the novel; this, together with the realization that we are not so repeatedly reminded of the religious affiliations of any of the other characters, makes Fitzgerald's description of Wolfsheim take on added significance. It is important to note, too, that Wolfsheim as yet has done nothing evil, but it is clear that his name, his "tiny eyes," his "large head," and "the two fine growths of hair which luxuriated in either nostril," serve to emphasize Wolfsheim's animalistic qualities and to arouse in the reader feelings of repulsion and abhorrence.

Wolfsheim's materialism is emphasized by his cufflinks that are made out of human molars:

"I see you're looking at my cuff buttons."

I hadn't been looking at them, but I did now. They were composed of oddly familiar pieces of ivory.

"Finest specimens of human molars," he informed me.

The fact that the question as to whether these molars are his own or someone else's is never answered not only brings to mind the ethics of the usurer, but also hints at the combination of usury with the crimes of mutilation and cannibalism as was done in Shakespeare.

Several other aspects of the stereotype are fulfilled in this short scene. Wolfsheim speaks with an obvious speech impediment: "He went to Oggsford College in England. You know Oggsford College?" His deference in describing Gatsby as "the kind of man you'd like to take home and introduce to your mother and sister," is hardly strong enough to cover up the scorn he feels toward Gatsby: "I raised him up out of nothing, right out of the gutter." Consider how closely related this is to the stereotyped picture of the Jew's abomination for the Christian we cited above.

The animal-like characteristics of Wolfsheim are especially emphasized by Fitzgerald. His name, of course, is an obvious key, but note, too, that many other bestial traits such as eating with "ferocious delicacy," for example, are given to Wolfsheim. Fitzgerald spends a great deal of time talking about Wolfsheim's nose although it is very subtly done. He "covers Gatsby with his expressive nose," like an animal smelling his prey. Before Wolfsheim speaks to him, Carraway says, "His nostrils turned to me in an interested way," again suggesting the image of the animal smelling his prey before the kill. When Wolfsheim leaves the luncheon meeting, "his tragic nose was trembling." Like an animal, then, Wolfsheim seems to use his nose in a way essential to his existence.

The next time we see Wolfsheim is after Gatsby's death, and Fitzgerald takes the opportunity to further the stereotype. We have an emphasis on the secrecy in Wolfsheim's living habits with the reference to his name "not being in the phone book." The mysteriousness of Wolfsheim's business is strongly focused upon, thus abetting the concept of Wolfsheim as wizard. The spider sitting in the center of his web is analogous to Wolfsheim at the center of his phantom-like business operation about which no one knows anything. One point is clear, however, the Swastika Holding Company is up to no good.

Our final picture of Wolfsheim occurs after Gatsby's death; Wolfsheim is describing Gatsby as a young man. Here the picture of the innocent Gatsby is sharply contrasted with the portrait of the Jew villain as Wolfsheim's knife is now poised for the purpose of extortion. At this point Wolfsheim also represents the cowardly Jew, covering his cowardice with Talmudic logic: "When a man gets killed I never liked to get mixed up in it in any way. I keep out. Let us learn to show our friendship for a man when he is alive and not after he is dead."

Wolfsheim has a subordinate and yet very important role to play in the novel. Like the classical usurer, he is the power behind the scenes in Gatsby's life. We have his own statement in the closing passages of the novel that he not only "started" Gatsby, he "made him." There is no reason to doubt his word. A man who could play with the faith of fifty million people could surely make one yokel into a clean-limbed Romantic American whose refinement he could use in some mysterious way. However, despite his importance to the novel, Wolfsheim remains a caricature, a flatly-drawn figure who never takes on the three-dimensional qualities necessary in the portrayal of a real flesh-and-blood character. Wolfsheim does not succeed as a real Jew, for he does not succeed as a real man. In Wolfsheim's case the stereotype is carried so far that he is almost an allegorical figure, posessing no real humanity. Fitzgerald needed an evil manipulator; the villainous Jew served his purpose well.

The character of Robert Cohn, the Jew in *The Sun Also Rises*, is in the tradition of the classic Jewish type, the "shlemiel." But he fails as a Jewish character basically because he fails to be a genuine and consistently drawn "shlemiel." Not that Hemingway failed to give Cohn many of the classical attributes of the shlemiel. On the contrary, these attributes are present to such an extent that his derivation from the shlemiel is unmistakable.

The notion of the shlemiel is a rather complex one beginning with Talmudic commentaries. It is here that he is first considered a cuckold. Gradually, through medieval and Renaissance literature, the shlemiel became the stock figure and object of humor in Jewish folk tales.

Perhaps the best description of the shlemiel comes from Ibn Ezra (1092–1167), the Hebrew-Spanish poet, who talks about himself in a series of personal epigrams: "If I should undertake to sell candles the sun would never set; if I should deal in shrouds, no one would ever die." Through these expressions we have a combination of a kind of ironic humor and bitterness, and also perhaps a notion of the absurd.

It is from these these roots that shlemiel gradually became the stock figure and object of humor in Jewish folk tales. This clumsy, unfortunate, and ineffectual character appeared in a variety of forms, perhaps as an outright cuckold or a duped and henpecked husband, who was repeatedly defeated in sexual matters until "defeat had become his trademark." Coexistent with the humor that this figure elicits, there is a sense of the tragic about the shlemiel, for he is usually the cause of his own misfortune. He is not merely a victim of circumstance who has somehow missed that mark. He is at the same time guilty of some nebulous and tragic flaw and doomed to live under an unlucky star. These flaws remain nebulous, perhaps for the reason that stories about the shlemiel were "almost never psychological; a person was a shlemiel by virtue of what he did, not by what he thought."

In viewing Cohn as a shlemiel, an obvious beginning can be made with his sexual life. The themes of Cohn as cuckold and as henpecked lover are fully developed in the novel. Other shlemiel attributes brought out are Cohn's passivity, his failure to articulate, and his inability to cope with his more articulate and more aggressive companions. In effect, they become Cohn the man, not one to be taken seriously, but rather one who must be scorned and ridiculed. His "pitiful" and "sad Jewish face," "forever suffering," plagues the other characters. In other words, Cohn's Jewishness (which at one point in the novel is characterized by his pushing away a dish of cucumbers in favor of a plate of pickled herring) and its concomitant characteristics (real and imagined) are a source of irritation to Jake and the others. They see in him the archetypal Jew, the shlemiel, the misfit with "a big wreath of twisted garlic around his neck and on his chest," who, by asking the wrong questions and making the wrong comments, consistently violates the unwritten code of conduct adhered to by his companions.

This last point bears upon Cohn's final link with the traditional shlemiel. The shlemiel "became a point of reference for the community around him, . . . and as the 'fool,' he was free to criticize in a way that the others were not." Cohn too takes all of life with more than just "one grain of salt," and thus his presence serves as a satiric comment on the fundamental belief of his companions that their lives have a semblance of order, and a reminder of their colossal failure. It is only Cohn who would be able to say: "I can't stand it to think my life is going so fast and I'm not really living it." The fact that the others are condemned to live within the margins of the rules and with the sham of sophistication makes them unable to show any intensity of passion.

As a case in point, consider how Cohn unashamedly exhibits his love for Brett in spite of the fact that the code demands that one be cavalier about his love affairs. In contrast to Cohn's uninhibited crying, the code required that the show of love must exhibit itself as it does in Mike: "Isn't she a lovely piece? Don't you think so, Jake?" To the extent that Cohn stands outside this artificial code of conduct, he is superior in human terms to his successful persecutors. Thus, a genuine possibility in interpreting Cohn's personality is to see him as a social commentator, somewhat beyond the pale of the peculiar society in which he functioned, and somewhat superior to it.

On the other hand, in depicting Cohn as a shlemiel, Hemingway may have been attempting to characterize the lack of heroism of his generation. Basically the idea of using the shlemiel to serve this purpose is a workable one. For in an age which found itself unable to think in terms of the old-style hero, the figure of the shlemiel fits in well, blending as we have already noted, disparate elements of the comic and the tragic. In a very real sense, then, he becomes a natural candidate to serve as a metaphor of the human experience in modern times.

In adopting (perhaps inadvertently) the tradition of the shlemiel for *The Sun Also Rises*, Hemingway had confronted himself with an unusual opportunity either to make meaningful social commentary or to develop insights concerning the condition of man. Unfortunately Hemingway did not make successful use of this opportunity, and his failure to do so is intimately bound up with his failure to capture in Cohn the shlemiel's real essence. For, in spite of Hemingway's ingenious portrayal, Cohn remains an authentic shlemiel.

The difficulty in the depiction of Cohn as a shlemiel arises from several different sources. The first and lesser of these is Cohn's family background and his social and economic position in life. A shlemiel simply does not emerge from a wealthy New York family; nor does he attend Princeton; and most especially he does not become a collegiate boxing champion. All of these things Cohn has done. The true shlemiel comes from a humble background and is singularly unsuccessful in all of his ventures in life, including, by the way, those in his childhood. Cohn's sudden confrontation with his Jewishness at age eighteen which then evoked feelings of inferiority leading to shlemiel-like behavior, is simply not an adequate explanation.

The really significant failing of Cohn as shlemiel is his lack of charm. Although this might seem at first to be a minor matter it in fact is one of great importance. For the true shlemiel has as a major redeeming quality a charm and a "humaneness which makes him dangerously warm and lovable" at the same time that he is a social irritant who stands outside of the social structure and mores of the society in which he moves. A good part of the shlemiel's charm derives from his traditional ability to make humorous commentary on his own ineptitude, thus making ambivalent the attitude of society toward him. Cohn does not indulge in humorous commentary and, we feel, he would be totally unable to do so. For he lacks the lightness of touch, the "ironic posture to face a world he cannot beat or quit," the ability to laugh at himself that would make this possible.

This failing in Cohn's portrayal can be better appreciated through a brief comparison with a rather recent, but already classical, shlemiel, I. Bashevis Singer's, "Gimpel the Fool." Gimpel is a thoroughgoing shlemiel, a fool, who, in his own words has been labelled, "imbecile, donkey, flax-head, dope, glump, ninny, and fool," by the people of the *shtetl*. However, in the final analysis his foolishness triumphs over the wisdom of the world. For he affirms life with an ironic positivism and a bitter humor, expressed in part through "symbolic shrugs and gestures," that reflect an acceptance of his absurd condition in this world and perhaps a confidence that things might be better in the "next world." This is a remarkable quality in a man who was at the very bottom of the social scale within a society that was itself under great external pressure and upon which "the heaviest weights of history descended." Herein lies his great charm and his saving grace. This is the source of his ultimate triumph.

In the case of Cohn the *shtetl* has been replaced by the society of his companions. Like Gimpel, Cohn is a fool who occupies the lowest position within this society. But Cohn fails to share in Gimpel's redeeming ironic humor. Gimpel's "symbolic shrugs and gestures" are unknown to him. The source of Gimpel's triumph is inaccessible to him and in the end he remains a miserable failure.

Disparate though they are, Wolfsheim and Cohn share, besides their religion, the distinction of being the most repulsive characters in the novels in which they appear. Since we have condemned both of them as inauthentic Jews it is important to emphasize that we do not intend to imply that a "real" Jew must be morally upright or likeable. We can elucidate this point by briefly diverting our attention from Fitzgerald and Hemingway.

Bloch is one of the most faithfully portrayed of the Jewish characters in Proust's *A la recherche du temps perdu*. As in Hemingway and Fitzgerald this Jew commands attention for two reasons: first, he gives to the novel a very definite social significance; secondly, he acts as a catalytic agent upon the other characters of the novel and upon its narrator. But the point of difference between Bloch and the Jews in Hemingway and Fitzgerald is that the Jewishness of Bloch is not given "any extra-social dimension" which might detract from his importance as a social being. In other words, Proust has seen Bloch "chiefly as a component of the society he depicts." Bloch offends us the moment he appears in the novel, just as do several other characters in the novel, but not because they belong to any national or racial group. In other words, the fact that Bloch is an abhorrent Jew is not more important than the fact that he is an abhorrent man, in the same way that Swann's positive character does not take on added significance because he is a Jew. Thus Proust's Jews are not left hanging in midair. Rather, Proust provides a milieu that saves them from becoming stereotypes.

This social milieu has not been provided by Hemingway and Fitzgerald for Cohn and Wolfsheim. If these Jews are to be an integral part of the society which is being depicted, we may legitimately question the necessity to label them so emphatically as Jews. Since their Jewishness is obviously not central to the novels in which they appear, we should question the emphasis placed upon it. It can be conjectured that for Hemingway and Fitzgerald the traits of meanness, corruption, and weakness are somehow closely bound up with Jewishness. Partly for this reason, and partly because of the existing stereotypes, creating Cohn and Wolfsheim as Jews and emphasizing their Jewishness was a natural and convenient way for Hemingway and Fitzgerald to proceed. It was undoubtedly the way in which they felt they could most effectively achieve the character portraits they sought.

Hemingway's Morality of Compensation

Scott Donaldson

> *Books should be about the people you know, that you love and hate, not about the people you study up about. If you write them truly they will have all the economic implications a book can hold.*
>
> ERNEST HEMINGWAY

While voyaging back to the United States in 1833, Ralph Waldo Emerson puzzled over a definition of morals. His thoughts, he admitted in his journal, were "dim and vague," but one might obtain "some idea of them . . . who develops the doctrine in his own experience that nothing can be given or taken without an equivalent." In Emerson's sublime optimism, he weighted the scales of equivalence in favor of the taker. Only the half blind, as he observes in his essay on "The Tragic," had never beheld the House of Pain, which like the salt sea encroached on man in his felicity. But felicity was man's customary state, for he lived on the land, not at sea. If pain disturbed him, he could rest in the conviction that nature would proportion "her defence to the assault" and "that the intellect in its purity, and the moral sense in its purity, are not distinguished from each other, and both ravish us into a region whereinto these passionate clouds of sorrow cannot rise."

On this issue, Emerson's Concord voice sounds in off-key opposition to that of Emily Dickinson in western Massachusetts, who wrote of the primacy of pain in the equation of compensation:

From *American Literature* 43, no. 3 (November 1971). © 1971 by Duke University Press.

> For each extatic instant
> We must an anguish pay
> In keen and quivering ratio
> To the extasy
>
> For each beloved hour
> Sharp pittances of years—
> Bitter contested farthings—
> And Coffers heaped with Tears!

For her, the transactions of life have been costly; cosmic usurers demand payments of anguish, at unconscionable interest, for each momentary joy. But it is a debt that *"must"* be paid, however unfair the terms.

Ernest Hemingway, throughout his fiction but especially in *The Sun Also Rises*, sides with Dickinson in this hypothetical quarrel. The cost of joy, ecstasy, or happiness comes high, yet it must be met. Like the poet from Amherst, he expressed his view of compensation in the metaphor of finance—a metaphor which runs through the fabric of his first novel like a fine, essential thread, a thread so fine, indeed, that it has not before been perceived. The classical statement against Hemingway's lack of moral sensitivity in this book was made by James T. Farrell, who described the characters as "people who have not fully grown up" and the moral outlook as amounting "to the attitude that an action is good if it makes one feel good." Among others, even the perceptive Philip Young seems at first (later, he changed his mind) to have read *The Sun Also Rises* in this way: "Jake's disability excepted, always, the book now seems really the long *Fiesta* it was called in the English edition, and one's net impression today is of all the fun there is to be had in getting good and lost." That was not the impression clearly, that Hemingway meant to convey. Lunching with a group of professors from the University of Hawaii in 1941, he advised against their students reading *A Farewell to Arms*. "That's an immoral book. Let them read *The Sun Also Rises*. It's very moral.

It is Jake Barnes who explicitly states the code of Hemingway's "very moral" novel. Lying awake at Pamplona, Jake reflects that in having Brett for a friend, he "had been getting something for nothing" and that sooner or later he would have to pay the bill, which always came:

> I thought I had paid for everything. Not like the woman
> pays and pays. No idea of retributions or punishment. Just

exchange of values. You gave up something and got something else. Or you worked for something. You paid some
way for everything that was any good. I paid my way into
enough things that I liked, so that I had a good time. Either
you paid by learning about them, or by experience, or by
taking chances, or by money. Enjoying living was learning
to get your money's worth and knowing when you had it.
You could get your money's worth. The world was a good
place to buy in.

It is understandable that Jake, sexually crippled in the war, should
think that he has already paid for everything; and it is an index of his
maturity, as a man "fully grown up," that he comes to realize that he
may still have debts outstanding, to be paid, most often and most
insistently, in francs and pesetas and pounds and dollars.

For Jake's philosophical musing is illustrated time and again in the
profuse monetary transactions of *The Sun Also Rises*. On the second
page of the novel, one discovers that Robert Cohn has squandered
most of the $50,000 that his father, from "one of the richest Jewish
families in New York," has left him; on the last page of the book, that
Jake has tipped the waiter (the amount is unspecified) who has called a
taxi for him and Brett in Madrid. Between the beginning and the end,
Hemingway specifically mentions sums of money, and what they have
been able to purchase, a total of thirty times. The money dispensed
runs up from a franc to a waiter to the fifty francs that Jake leaves for
his *poule*, Georgette, at the dancings, to the two hundred francs which
Count Mippipopolous gives to Jake's concierge, to the $10,000 the
count offers Brett for a weekend in her company. Mostly, though,
the monetary amounts are small, and pay for the food, drink, travel,
and entertainment that represent the good things in life available to
Jake.

Hemingway reveals much more about his characters' financial
condition and spending habits than about their appearance: the book
would be far more useful to the loan officer of a bank than, say, to the
missing person's bureau, which would have little more physical infor-
mation to go on, with respect to height, weight, hair and eye color,
than that Brett had short hair and "was built with curves like the hull
of a racing yacht" and that Robert Cohn, with his broken nose, looked
as if "perhaps a horse had stepped on his face." When Hemingway cut
40,000 words out of the first draft of *The Sun Also Rises* but retained

these ubiquitous references to the cost of things, he must have kept them for some perceptible and important artistic purpose.

II

In fact, he had several good reasons to note with scrupulous detail the exact nature of financial transactions. Such a practice contributed to the verisimilitude of the novel, denoting the way it was; it fitted nicely with Jake's—and his creator's—obsession with the proper way of doing things; and mainly, it illustrated in action the moral conviction that you must pay for what you get, that you must earn in order to be able to buy, and that only then will it be possible, if you are careful, to buy your money's worth in the world.

In the early 1920s exchange rates in postwar Europe fluctuated wildly. Only the dollar remained stable, to the benefit of the expatriated artists, writers, dilettantes, and party-goers who found they could live for next to nothing in Paris. Malcolm Cowley and his wife lived there the year of 1921 in modest comfort on a grant of $1,000, twelve thousand francs by that year's rate. By the summer of 1924, when Barnes and his companions left for the fiesta at Pamplona, the rate was still more favorable, almost 19 francs to the dollar. And you could get breakfast coffee and a brioche for a franc or less at the cafés where Hemingway, expatriated with the rest, wrote when the weather turned cold. There were even better bargains elsewhere, and the Hemingways, somewhat strapped once Ernest decided to abandon journalism for serious fiction, found one of the best of them in the winter of 1924–25, at Schruns in the Austrian Voralberg, where food, lodging, snow and skiing for the young writer, his wife, and son came to but $28.50 a week. Europe was overflowing with (mostly temporary) American expatriates, living on the cheap. Any novel faithful to that time and that place was going to have to take cognizance of what it cost to live and eat and drink.

Hemingway regarded most of his fellow Americans on the Left Bank as poseurs pretending to be artists, but "nearly all loafers expending the energy that an artist puts into his creative work in talking about what they are going to do and condemning the work of all artists who have gained any degree of recognition." The tone of moral indignation in this dispatch, one of the first that Hemingway sent the *Toronto Star Weekly* from Paris in 1922, is emphasized by the anecdote he includes about "a big, light-haired woman sitting at a table with three young men." She pays the bill, and the young men laugh whenever she does: "Three years ago she came to Paris with her husband from a little town in Connecticut, where they had lived and he had painted with increasing success for ten years. Last year he went back to America alone."

To the writer, single-minded in his dedication to his craft, the time-wasting of café habitués represented the greatest sin of all. It was the work that counted, and talking about art was hardly a satisfactory substitute. As Jake remarks, setting forth an axiom of Hemingway's creed, "You'll lose it if you talk about it." In the posthumously published *A Moveable Feast*, Hemingway laments have accompanied the hypochondriacal Scott Fitzgerald on an unnecessarily drawn-out trip to Lyon. Nursing his traveling companion, he "missed not working and . . . felt the death loneliness that comes at the end of every day that is wasted in your life." Observing the playboys and playgirls of Paris waste their lives on one long hazy binge, Hemingway as foreign correspondent felt much the same disgust that visits Jake after the revels at Pamplona, when he plunges deep into the waters off San Sebastian in an attempt to cleanse himself.

What distinguishes Jake Barnes from Mike and Brett, who at least make no pretenses toward artistic (or any other kind of) endeavor, and from Robert Cohn, a writer who is blocked throughout the novel, is that he works steadily at his regular job as a newspaperman. He is, presumably, unsupported by money from home, and he spends his money, as he eats and drinks, with conspicuous control. Above all, he is thoughtful and conscientious in his spending. Sharing a taxi with two fellow American reporters who also work regularly and well at their jobs but at least one of whom is burdened, as he is not, by "a wife and kids," Jake insists on paying the two-franc fare. He does the right thing, too, by Georgette, the streetwalker he picks up at the Napolitain. Not only does he buy her dinner as a preliminary to the sexual encounter she has bargained for, but upon deserting her for Brett, he leaves fifty francs with the patronne—compensation for her wasted evening—to be delivered to Georgette if she goes home alone. The patronne is supposed to hold the money for Jake if Georgette secures another male customer, but this being France, he will, Brett assures him, lose his fifty francs. "Oh, yes," Jake responds, but he has at least behaved properly, and Jake, like his creator, was "always intensely interested in how to do a thing," from tying flies to fighting bulls to compensating a prostitute. Besides, he shares a double kinship with

Georgette: she too is sick, a sexual cripple, and she pursues her trade openly and honestly.

The case is different with Lady Ashley, who acquires and casts off her lovers nearly as casually as Georgette, but does so without thought of the consequences to others. There is a certain irony in Brett's telling Jake that it was wrong of him to bring Georgette to the dance, "in restraint of trade." Surely this is a case of the pot and kettle, for she has arrived in the company of a covey of homosexuals. More to the point, it is women like Brett—and even, to a lesser degree, Cohn's companion Frances Clyne—who provide unfair competition to the streetwalkers of Paris.

After an unsatisfactory time with Brett, Jake Barnes returns to his room, where he immediately goes over his bank statement: "It showed a balance of $2,432.60. I got out my checkbook and deducted four checks drawn since the first of the month, and discovered I had a balance of $1,832.60. I wrote this on the back of the statement." This is a make-work, an attempt to delay thinking about the love for Brett that he cannot consummate. But it is also characteristic of Jake's meticulousness about money. The surprising thing, in fact, is that Jake should have spent as much as $600 in any given month, for he is a man who tries very hard always to get his money's worth. He knows whom to write to secure good bullfight tickets, and he reserves the best rooms in the best hotels at the best price. In Bayonne, he helps Bill buy "a pretty good rod cheap, and two landing-nets," and checks with the tourist-office "to find what we ought to pay for a motor-car to Pamplona": 400 francs. At Burguete, he bargains to have the wine included in the twelve-pesetas-a-day hotel room he and Bill share, and they make certain at dinner that they do "not lose money on the wine." He is annoyed when Cohn sends a wire of only three words for the price of ten ("I come Thursday"), and takes revenge by answering with an even shorter telegram ("Arriving to-night"). After the fiesta, when a driver tries to overcharge Jake for a ride from Bayonne to San Sebastian, he first works the price down from fifty to thirty-five pesetas and then rejects that price too, as "not worth it." Jake is careful to fulfill his obligations, but he will not be taken advantage of. Once, in church, regretting that he is such a rotten Catholic, he even prays that he will "make a lot of money," but here the verb is important, for he next begins thinking about how he might make the money. He does not pray or even hope to *have* a lot of money, or for it to descend upon him from the trees or the deaths of relatives. Robert Cohn and Mike Campbell remind him, often and painfully, of what inherited money, or the promise of it, can do to undermine a man.

III

Though physically impotent and mentally tortured, Jake Barnes remaines morally sound, while Mike Campbell, Robert Cohn, and Brett Ashley, who are physically whole, have become morally decadent. As Baker observes, *The Sun Also Rises* has "a sturdy moral backbone," deriving much of its power from the contrast between Barnes-Gorton-Romero, who constitute the "moral norm" of the book, and the morally aberrant trio of Ashley-Campbell-Cohn. What has not been observed is that money and its uses form the metaphor by which the moral responsibility of Jake, Bill, and Pedro is measured against the carelessness of Brett, Mike, and Robert. Financial soundness mirrors moral strength.

Bill Gorton is the most likeable of the crew at the fiesta. Modeled upon the humorist Donald Ogden Stewart, Bill regales Jake with topical gags about Mencken, the Scopes trial, literary fashions, and middle-class mores. An enthusiast, he finds every place he visits equally "wonderful." The adjective is a private joke between Barnes and Gorton, for Bill knows as well as Jake that when things are really wonderful, it is neither necessary nor desirable to say so. Thus, hiking through the magnificent woods at Burguete, Bill remarks simply, "This is country." The five days they share at Burguete stand in idyllic contrast to the sickness and drunkenness which characterize both Paris and Pamplona. It is not that Bill and Jake do not drink together on the fishing trip; they drink prodigious quantities of wine. But it is drinking for the pleasure they have earned, both through hard work (in contrast to Cohn, Gorton is a producing writer) and through the rigors of the outdoor life they choose to pursue on vacation. Furthermore, Bill knows when not to drink. After dinner at Madame Lecomte's and a long walk through Paris, Jake proposes a drink. "No," says Bill. "I don't need it."

The first thing Jake says about Bill Gorton is that he is "very happy. He had made a lot money on his last book, and was going to make a lot more." He has paid for his fiesta, and like all who have earned "the good things," he is careful of the rights of others. In Vienna, he tells Jake, he had gone to an "enormous . . . prize-fight" in which a "wonderful nigger" knocked a local boy cold and aroused the anger of the crowd. People threw chairs into the ring, and not only was the victorious fighter deprived of payment (he had agreed not to knock out the local fighter), but his watch was stolen. "Not so good, Jake. Injustice everywhere," as Gorton remarks. Conscientious about money matters, he is disturbed by a world where fights are fixed and debts go unpaid. So, though tight and on holiday, Bill lends the cheated fighter clothes and money and tries to help him collect what's owed to him.

Bill's comic determination to purchase stuffed animals foreshadows Jake's serious reflections on compensation. Passing a Paris taxidermist's, Bill appeals to Jake to buy

> "Just one stuffed dog. I can take 'em or leave 'em alone.
> But listen, Jake. Just one stuffed dog."
> "Come on."
> "Mean everything in the world to you after you bought
> it. Simple exchange of values. You give them money. They
> give you a stuffed dog."

His affinity for spending money on the ridiculous emerges again at Pamplona, when he buys Mike eleven shoeshines in a row. "Bill's a yell of laughter," Mike says, but Jake, who unlike them has not had much to drink, "felt a little uncomfortable about all this shoe-shining." Still, Bill's expenditures buy amusement for himself and others (including, of course, the reader), and these otherwise merely amusing incidents serve to illustrate the principle of exchange of values: to obtain stuffed dogs, shoeshines, or drinks, you must deliver payment.

IV

Robert Cohn, for whom Gorton conceives an immediate dislike, does not belong with the party at Pamplona. A romantic, he is understandably unable at first to conceive that his weekend with Brett at San Sebastian has meant nothing to her, but he forfeits any claim to sympathy by his subsequent stubborn and violent unwillingness to accept that obvious fact. Terribly insecure, he takes insult after insult from Frances and Mike without retaliation, though he is ready enough, anachronistically, to fight with his "best friend" Jake over what he construes as insults to Brett. A Jew in the company of Gentiles, he is a bore who takes himself—and his illusions—far too seriously. Unlike

Jake, he has not "learned about" things. He does not know how to eat or drink or love. It is no wonder that Harold Loeb, unmistakably recognizing himself in Hemingway's portrait of Cohn, "felt as if he had developed an ulcer" and, decades later, attempted to vindicate himself in his autobiography.

Still, it would be possible to pity Cohn for his dominant malady (is not romantic egotism a less unlovely illness than nymphomania or dipsomania?) were it not for his callous and opportunistic use of the money he has not earned. His allowance ($300 a month, from his mother) comfortably stakes him to his period of expatriation. He has written a novel which has been "accepted by a fairly good publisher," but it is not, clearly, a very good novel, and now the well has run dry. In his idleness, he hangs around Jake's office, disturbing his work, and even proposes to pay Jake's way as his companion on a trip to South America, a continent he invests with an aura of romance. How Hemingway felt about such proposals was later made clear in *A Moveable Feast,* when he reflected, in connection with the trip to Lyon with Fitzgerald, that he "had been a damned fool to accept an invitation for a trip that was to be paid for by someone else." But biographical evidence is hardly necessary to make the point that Cohn, whose money comes to him through no effort of his own but fortuitously because of the accident of his birth, does not understand the proper way of spending it: the point is made implicitly by a number of incidents in *The Sun Also Rises.*

Having inherited a great deal of money, he has wasted nearly all of it on a little magazine—and in maintaining the prestige that came to him as its editor. He is consistently lucky in gambling, but that does him more harm than good. What comes too easily has a pernicious effect on him as a person. While he was in New York to see his publisher, for example, several women had been nice to him as a budding novelist.

> This changed him so that he was not so pleasant to have around. Also, playing for higher stakes than he could afford in some rather steep bridge games with his New York connections he has held cards and won several hundred dollars. It made him rather vain of his bridge game, and he talked several times of how a man could always make a living at bridge if he were ever forced to.

Cohn wins a 100-peseta bet with Gorton that Mike and Brett will not arrive as scheduled at Pamplona, but the bet costs him any possibility of friendship with Bill. Gorton wagers, in fact, only because Cohn's arrogance in parading inside knowledge of Brett's and Mike's habits makes him angry. Furthermore, when the wager has been agreed on, Cohn first does Bill the indignity of asking Jake to remember it, and then, to make amends after he has won, pretends that it really does not matter.

What most damns Cohn, however, is his habit of buying his way out of obligations to women. Frances Clyne, one of the bitchiest women in Hemingway's fiction, reveals this practice of Cohn's in a devastating scene. Flat broke and not so young or attractive as she once was, Frances is being packed off to England so that her paramour may see more of the world—and, he surely hopes, of Lady Ashley:

> "Robert's sending me. He's going to give me two hundred pounds [about a thousand dollars] and then I'm going to visit friends. Won't it be lovely? The friends don't know about it, yet."
>
> She turned to Cohn and smiled at him. He was not smiling now.
>
> "You were only going to give me a hundred pounds, weren't you, Robert? But I made him give me two hundred. You're really very generous. Aren't you, Robert?"

"I do not know," Jake reflects, "how people could say such terrible things to Robert Cohn." But Frances can say them, and get away with it, because they are absolutely true. Cohn, in fact, has disposed of another girl, his "little secretary on the magazine," in just the same way, except cheaper. It is in his attempt to buy his way out of entanglements, without expending anything of himself, that Robert Cohn most viciously breaks the moral code of compensation.

Furthermore, there are suggestions in the book that Cohn is tightfisted with his money. He has, apparently, tried to bargain with Frances. He directs Jake to buy him a double-tapered fishing line, but says he will pay later instead of now. After unleashing a stream of insults against Cohn ("Don't you know you're not wanted?"), Mike Campbell tells Bill Gorton, who is about to remove Cohn from the slaughter, to stay. "Don't go," Mike said. "Robert Cohn's about to buy a drink." The clear implication is that Robert Cohn rarely buys drinks.

Mike, on the other hand, is more than willing to buy drinks, whenever—which means rarely—he has any money. As is true of all the other major characters in the book, Hemingway reveals a good deal about Mike's financial condition and habits. Brett, Jake tells Robert, is going to marry Mike Campbell. "He's going to be rich as hell some day." Cohn refuses to believe that Brett will marry Mike—and indeed, the matter remains in doubt at the end of the novel—but there is no question about Mike's potential wealth. He is trying, Brett says, to get his mother to pay for her divorce so they can be married. "Michael's people have loads of money." But for the moment, he makes do on a rather skimpy allowance, and is not even allowed to write checks. When he needs funds, he must "send a wire to the keeper."

Mike Campbell is held under strict financial control for the best of reasons: he is totally irresponsible about money. With his anticipated future wealth serving as a promissory note, he sponges off everyone in sight and simply does not pay his debts. After suffering a business collapse, he has had to resort to bankruptcy, an ungentlemanly if legal way of evading creditors. It is, as Brett realizes when she introduces him, one of the two most important and typical things about the man she intends to marry. The other is that he drinks far too much: "This is Bill Gorton. This drunkard is Mike Campbell. Mr. Campbell is an undischarged bankrupt."

Mike is no more conscientious about settling his debts to friends than to his former business "connections." Yet he possesses a certain self-deprecatory wit, and Bill Gorton, especially, is drawn to him. Bill likes Mike so much, in fact, that it is very difficult for him to admit that Mike does not meet his obligations. One night in Pamplona, Mike, Bill, and Bill's girl Edna are thrown out of a bar by the police. "I don't know what happened," Bill says, "but some one had the police called to keep Mike out of the back room. There were some people that had known Mike at Cannes. What's the matter with Mike?" "Probably he owes them money," Jake says. "That's what people usually get bitter about." The next morning, Bill remembers the incident more clearly: "There was a fellow there that had helped pay Brett and Mike out of Cannes, once. He was damned nasty." The night before, Bill had emphatically defended his friend: "They can't say things like that about Mike." But in the light of dawn, he modifies the statement: "Nobody ought to have a right to say things about Mike. . . . They oughtn't to have any right. I wish to hell they didn't have any right." Bill's own loyalty to Mike finally crumbles when, after the fiesta, another incident makes it clear *why* they have the right.

Jake, Bill, and Mike have hired a car together, and stop at "a very Ritz place" in Biarritz where they roll dice to see who will pay for the drinks. Mike loses three times in a row, but cannot pay for the third round:

> "I'm so sorry," Mike said. "I can't get it."
> "What's the matter?"
> "I've no money," Mike said. "I'm stony. I've just twenty francs. Here, take twenty francs."
> Bill's face sort of changed.

He had had just enough money for his hotel bill in Pamplona, Mike explains, though it turns out that Brett has given him all of her cash to pay his bill. Neither can Mike help pay for their car, and his promise to send Jake what he owes is hardly reassuring.

Mike continually banters about his bankruptcy, as if making light of the obligations might somehow cause them to disappear. "I'm a tremendous bankrupt," he remarks. "I owe money to everybody." He will not go down into the ring after the running of the bulls because "it wouldn't be fair to my creditors." As Mike observes, "One never gets anywhere by discussing finances," but he is unable to resist touching the wound by discussing his own. There is the story, for example, of the medals and Mike's tailor. Invited to "a whopping big dinner" in England where medals are to be worn, Mike prevails upon his tailor to supply him with some medals which had been left by another customer for cleaning. When the dinner fizzles out, he goes to a nightclub and passes the medals around. "Gave one to each girl. Form of souvenir. They thought I was hell's own shakes of a soldier. Gave away medals in a night club. Dashing fellow." The story delights his audience, but it had not seemed so funny to his tailor. If it was foolish to set too great store by military medals, as did the chap who had left them with the tailor, it was quite wrong to propose to wear medals that one had not earned. Mike has fought in the war, and "must have some medals," but he does not know which ones and has never sent in for them. He is careless about them, quite as willing to don other people's ribbons as he is to spend other people's money.

Brett shares with Mike a carelessness of personal behavior which stems from a lifetime of having had things done for her. Her room in Madrid, for example, "was in that disorder produced only by those who have always had servants." She makes appointments and does not keep them. She accepts the generosity of others as if it were her due. The Paris homosexuals, one feels certain, were paying her way. Count Mippipopolous finances her champagne binge. "Come on," she says at Pamplona. "Are these poisonous things paid for?" In the bar of the Palace Hotel in Madrid, she asks Jake, "*Would* you buy a lady a drink?" She has been given, she admits, "hell's own amount of credit" on her title. And, of course, she and Mike had jointly run up the bills they could not settle at Cannes. Moreover, she satisfies her demanding sexual appetites at the expense of others, effectively turning Robert into a steer, Mike into a swine, and Jake into a pimp. She is clearly not what Madame Duzinell, Jake's concierge, calls her after the bribe of 200 francs from the count, "très, très gentille."

Oddly, though, Brett observes a strict code in connection with her sexual activity. She will not accept money for her favors. Thus she rejects the count's offer of "ten thousand dollars to go to Biarritz [or Cannes, or Monte Carlo] with him." She pays Mike's way, not vice versa, out of the Hotel Montoya. Though Romero pays the hotel bills in Madrid, she will take nothing else from him. "He tried to give me a lot of money, you know. I told him I had scads of it. He knew that was a lie. I couldn't take his money, you know." In sending Romero away, against the urgings of the flesh, she has done the right thing at the cost of real personal anguish. She will be neither a whore nor "one of those bitches that ruins children."

Furthermore, Brett's apparent nymphomania can be at least partly excused by the unhappy circumstances of her past life. She has lost one man she loved in the war, and married another ("Ashley, chap she got the title from") who has returned quite mad from serving as a sailor. "When he came home," Mike explains, "he wouldn't sleep in a bed. Always made Brett sleep on the floor. Finally, when he got really bad, he used to tell her he'd kill her. Always slept with a loaded service revolver. Brett used to take the shells out when he'd gone to sleep. She hasn't had an absolutely happy life." Like Jake, she still suffers from war wounds. Like him, too, she articulates her awareness of the law of compensation. If she has put chaps through hell, she's paying for it all now. "Don't we pay for all the things we do, though?"

Brett's case is far more ambiguous than that of Robert Cohn or Mike Campbell. If she recklessly imposes nearly insupportable burdens on others, she carries an even heavier burden herself. Morally, she is neither angel nor devil, but somewhere, rather fascinatingly, in between. It is almost as if Hemingway himself were alternately attracted to and repelled by Brett. In Carlos Baker's biography there is a strong implication that Hemingway either had, or wanted to have, an affair with Duff Twysden, the prototype for Brett. In the fall of 1925, Duff sent Hemingway a note asking for a loan: "Ernest my dear, forgive me for this effort but can you possibly lend me some money? I am in a stinking fix but for once only temporary and can pay you back for *sure*. I want 3,000 francs— but for Gods sake lend me as much as you can." In the novel, as if to protect Duff, Hemingway transfers her behavior to Mike Campbell: it is he and not Brett who asks, repeatedly, for loans.

V

Hemingway's insistence on the need to earn, and to pay for, what you get is in no way a statement in support of materialism, for it is accompanied by disgust with the crooked and corrupting values of the commercial world. Eager to line their pockets, the merchants of Pamplona double prices during the fiesta. Away go the café's marble-topped tables and comfortable white wicker chairs, to be replaced by cast-iron tables and severe folding chairs: "The café was like a battleship stripped for action." The warship's objective, of course, is to relieve peasants and tourists alike of their cash. At the start of the fiesta, the peasants confine their drinking to the outlying shops, where wine sells for 30 centimes a liter. "They had come in so recently from the plains and the hills that it was necessary that they make their shifting in values gradually. . . . Money still had a definite value in hours worked and bushels of grain sold. Late in the fiesta it would not matter what they paid, nor where they bought." When the peasants reach the stage of heedlessness (epitomized by the futile death of one of them during the running of the bulls), they will have lost any sense of the dignity of labor, of hours worked and bushels sold.

The cancer of commercialism also threatens to infect bullfighting. Romero is forced to face a dangerously bad bull, who cannot see well the lure of the cape, because the promoters have paid for the bull and "don't want to lose their money." The crowd sends a volley of cushions, bread, and vegetables into the ring where Belmonte, ill and more cautious than he once had been, is performing his art. "Belmonte was very good. But because he got thirty thousand pesetas and people had stayed in line all night to buy tickets to see him, the crowd demanded that he should be more than very good." His greatness had been "discounted and sold in advance," and nothing he could do would satisfy those who watched him do it.

Montoya, an aficionado who represents bullfighting's conscience, puts up all the good toreros at his hotel, and keeps in his room framed photographs of the bullfighters he "really believed in." The pictures of the commercial bullfighters, though, are consigned first to a desk drawer and then to the wastebasket. Montoya welcomes Jake, a fellow aficionado, and is grateful for his advice not to deliver to Romero his invitation from the American ambassador. "People take a boy like that," the hotel-keeper explains. "They don't know what he's worth. . . . They start this Grand Hotel business, and in one year they're through." Montoya is even inclined to forgive Jake his friends, but that tolerance dissolves when he sees "Pedro Romero with a big glass of cognac in his hand, sitting laughing between me [Jake] and a woman with bare shoulders, at a table full of drunks. He did not even nod." When Jake and his companions check out, Montoya does "not come near" them.

Romero, however, remains immune to the disease of commercialism—and the caution unto cowardice it is likely to breed. He wants and expects to make money as a bullfighter: when Brett reads in his hand that there are thousands of bulls in his future, "Good," he replies, and in an aside to Jake in Spanish, "At a thousand duros apiece." But he has not yet begun to compromise his bullfighting, as Belmonte has, by insisting on manageable bulls with smallish horns. And Hemingway invokes the metaphor of profit and loss in comparing Pedro's afternoon of triumph to the jeers that had greeted Belmonte: "Pedro Romero had the greatness. He loved bull-fighting, and I think he loved the bulls, and I think he loved Brett. Everything of which he could control the locality he did in front of her all that afternoon. . . . But he did not do it for her at any loss to himself. He gained by it all through the afternoon." His willingness to take chances, one of the ways, as Jake has reflected, in which you could pay "for everything that was any good," gives the bullfight, his relationship with Brett, and the fiesta itself a kind of dignity.

It hardly matters that "the Biarritz crowd" does not appreciate what he has accomplished, with either his bad bull or his good one. Hemingway obviously regards the rich English and American tourists from Biarritz, come for one day of the quaint fiesta at Pamplona, with undisguised scorn. Those who buy false wares, like the secretly manipulated boxer toys hawked on the streets of Paris, deserve no more than they get.

The depth of this contempt can be measured against the sympathetic portrayal of Wilson-Harris, the Englishman who fishes and plays three-handed bridge with Jake and Bill at Burguete. When his companions must leave, Harris (as the Americans call him) insists on buying them a bottle of wine apiece. The atmosphere is one of warm camaraderie, punctuated by Harris's regret that Bill and Jake must leave. As they board the bus for Pamplona, Harris presses still another gift upon each of them: a dozen flies that he has tied himself. "They're not first-rate flies at all," he insists. "I only thought if you fished them some time it might remind you of what a good time we had." It has been a good time indeed, so that Jake first wishes Harris were coming along to Pamplona but then reflects that "You couldn't tell how English would mix with each other, anyway." But you can tell: a man who spends his holiday trout fishing in the Pyrenees and who behaves so generously would not have mixed at all well with the perpetually carousing crew at the fiesta.

Hemingway's major characters in the novel are all, with the exception of Romero, English and American, and each is easily distinguishable from the others. The foreigners, though, he tends to stereotype. Most of the Europeans in the book are, of course, French or Spanish, and these two nationalities are characterized almost solely on the basis of their attitude toward money. French standards of value are epitomized by Jake's concierge, who will not admit shabbily dressed friends of Jake to his quarters and who conveniently changes her mind about Brett—from "a species of woman" to "a lady . . . of very good family"—on the strength of a bribe. In *The Sun Also Rises*, Frenchmen always have their hands out, like the dining-car conductor who pockets ten francs but does nothing to earn them. In an interior monologue, Jake dissects the French national character. He has just overtipped a waiter in Bayonne: "Everything is on such a clear financial basis in France. It is the simplest country to live in. No one makes things complicated by becoming your friend for any obscure reason. If you want people to like you you have only to spend a little money. I spent a little money and the waiter liked me. He appreciated my valuable qualities." Repetition and the pun on "valuable qualities" underscore the heavy irony of this passage. For Jake obviously prefers Spain to France, just as he prefers bullfighting, a sport which cannot be fixed, to Viennese prizefights and French and Belgian bicycle-racing where the contestants "had raced among themselves so often that it did not make much difference who won. . . . The money could be arranged."

Spaniards, unlike Frenchmen, were likely to be friendly for no good financial reason at all. The Basques, for example, share a crowded bus with Bill and Jake, and all share their wine, the Americans from bottles they have just bought, the Spanish from their wineskins. When the bus stops at a *posada* in a small town, Bill and Jake each have an *aguardiente*, at twenty centimes apiece. "I gave the woman fifty centimes to make a tip, and she gave me back the copper piece, thinking I had misunderstood the price." Two of the Basques join them, and the cost of the drinks is split equally between them. On the opening day of the fiesta at Pamplona, Spanish peasants in a wine-shop will not let Jake and his friends pay for wine and food. They will accept in return only "a rinse of the mouth from the new wine-bag" Jake has bought, at the "lowest price," because the shopkeeper discovers he intends to drink out of it, not resell it in Bayonne. Spanish peasants, with their ethic of sharing, display a dignity and readiness for fellowship not to be thought of among the French.

The minor character who best exemplifies the morality of compensation is the Greek Count Mippipopolous. It is possible to regard him solely as the sort of aging voluptuary that he appears, on the surface, to be. But to do so is to miss the point. It "means any amount to him" to buy fine champagne directly from Baron Mumms. All he wants out of wines, he says, is to enjoy them. When Brett objects to his ordering a bottle of 1811 brandy, he reprimands her in his customary tough English:

> "Listen, my dear. I get more value for my money in old
> brandy than in any other antiquities."
> "Got many antiquities?"
> "I got a houseful."

It is the same with food, and with women: the count can enjoy them properly because he has a sense of values acquired through long and painful experience. Count Mippipopolous has been involved in seven wars and four revolutions. In Abyssinia when he was twenty-one, two arrows went clean through his body: he shows Brett and Jake the scars. He is "one of us," as she remarks after this demonstration, because like them he has paid in suffering for the pleasures he now pursues. The temptation to judge the count by puritanical standards (Jake last sees him at Zelli's, surrounded by three girls he has just picked up) is tempered by an awareness that he has earned his pleasure, and that generosity and loyalty, as well as hedonism, from facets of his code.

VI

After delivering himself of his thoughts on the need to pay for the good things, Jake Barnes concludes rather cynically, "It seemed like a fine philosophy. In five years . . . it will seem just as silly as all the other fine philosophies I've had." Hemingway, however, did not abandon the code of compensation Jake had enunciated, but continued to regard the rich—and the lure of easy money—as threats to artists in general and himself in particular. Money, he wrote John Dos Passos in 1929, "had been the ruination of too many of their friends. Don Stewart had taken up with Jock Whitney, to say nothing of selling his soul to Hollywood for a $25,000 contract. John Bishop's career had been spoiled by his wife's munificent income. The search of eternal youth had clearly sunk the Fitzgeralds. In *Green Hills of Africa*, he cited money as the first way in which American writers are destroyed. When they have made some money, they "increase their standard of living and they are caught. They have to write to keep up their establishments, their wives, and so on, and they write slop."

For his own part, as becomes clear in *A Moveable Feast*, he quite specifically blamed the demise of his idyllic first marriage on the predatory rich who had followed Hadley, Bumby, and himself to the Voralberg:

> When you have two people who love each other, are happy and gay and really good work is being done by one or both of them, people are drawn to them. . . . Those who attract people . . . do not always learn about the good, the attract-ive, the charming, the soon-beloved, the generous, the understanding rich who have no bad qualities and who give each day the quality of a festival and who, when they have passed and taken the nourishment they needed, leave every-thing deader than the roots of any grass Attila's horses' hoofs have ever scoured.

Especially in the long story *The Snows of Kilimanjaro*. Hemingway excoriated himself, in the guise of the writer-narrator Harry, for drink-ing and playing with the rich and letting his talent erode through idleness. "It was strange, too, wasn't it," Harry thinks, "that when he fell in love with another woman, that woman should always have more money than the last one." That was exactly the case with Pauline, Hemingway's second wife, and as Philip Young has divined, the story is partly "a special and private . . . analysis of his past failures as a writer of prose fiction, as of 1936." He had not published a first-rate book since *A Farewell to Arms*, seven years before, and like Harry, contemplated with despair all the stories he had not written. Though it was not really his wife's fault, though he had destroyed his talent himself, still it was her money that gave him the chance to spend what he had not earned and was not paying for. Perhaps it was not coincidental that in his other major fiction of the 1930s, Hemingway depicted his most coolly vicious female characters of all in Margot Macomber and Helene Bradley, the rich, writer-collecting adventuress of *To Have and Have Not*.

But the morality of compensation found expression not only in the fiction of the thirties, but throughout Hemingway's works. Both in *A Farewell to Arms* (1929) and *Across the River and into the Trees* (1950), his protagonists are virtually obsessed with their obligations. After making his "separate peace" with the war, a totally justifiable escape, Frederic Henry nonetheless feels "damned lonely" and tortures himself with recurring thoughts that he has deserted in a conventional way. Colonel Cantwell, facing his certain death, carefully discharges his outstanding debts: he sends ducks to the waiter at the Gritti Palace Hotel, returns his girl's emeralds and her portrait, and makes her a gift of the shotguns that have served him so well. All of Hemingway's major protagonists share this sense of obligation—to political belief (Robert Jordan), to craft (Santiago as well as Romero), to wife and family (Harry Morgan). Though Hemingway himself was divorced three times, his heroes never cast off commitments. They pay their bills in full, sometimes at the cost of their lives.

A teacher in Oak Park, Illinois, an upper-middle-class suburb noted for nothing so much as its respectability, once wondered "how a boy brought up in Christian and Puritan nurture should know and write so well of the devil and the underworld." But Ernest Hemingway carried with him always an inheritance from the community where he grew up, a faith in the efficacy and staying power of certain moral values. Strongest among these was the axiom that you had to earn your happiness, though the price might come exceedingly high, with its corollary that easy money could ruin a man. In his first novel, Hemingway imposed this standard on the expatriate world of the early

1920s. At the end of the last book he wrote, looking back on those years as an idyl when he had worked hard and loved well and taken nothing without making full payment, his nostalgia found expression in the same metaphor which runs through *The Sun Also Rises:* "Paris was always worth it and you received return for whatever you brought to it. But this is how it was in the early days when we were very poor and very happy."

The End of *The Sun Also Rises:* A New Beginning

Carole Gottlieb Vopat

While some critics, most notably Philip Young, feel that Jacob Barnes does not change at all in the course of *The Sun Also Rises,* and others, like Mark Spilka, John Rouch, and Richard Hovey, conclude that Jake changes only to realize the full extent of his inability to change, a close critical reading of the end of the novel indicates that this position needs to be reevaluated. Jake Barnes does indeed undergo profound change, and that change, which has taken place gradually and progressively throughout the novel, is summed up concisely and symbolically in the final pages of book 3.

Jake has undergone the shock of many recognitions before book 3 opens. He has been changed by the events in Pamplona: the spectacle of Romero's utter masculinity; the revelation of his own shameful role as steer and pimp; the realization that he is in his romantic dreaming little different, although quieter, than Robert Cohn. More importantly, he has recognized that what he had been calling romantic love is instead compulsion and misery, a neurotic and scarcely uncontrollable sickness which, rather than shore up his tentative masculinity, only serves to castrate him further. Jake has changed in his estimation of himself, his wound, his crowd, and his love for Brett Ashley, who he has been discovering is not so "absolutely fine and straight."

In Paris Jake once accused Brett of liking "to add them up"; when she agreed ("Well, what if I do?"), he responded, "Nothing." In

From *Fitzgerald/Hemingway Annual, 1972,* edited by Matthew J. Bruccoli and C. E. Frazer Clark, Jr. © 1973 by the National Cash Register Company, Dayton, Ohio.

Pamplona, however, when Brett reveals her feelings about Romero (chapter 16), Jake is not as warmly accepting of her behavior. He has learned too much about himself and her to accept the myth or excuse of their specialness. When Brett refers to their mutual illusion—that their affair, could it materialize, would be perfect—he contradicts her: "I'd be as big an ass as Cohn." He sees that to Brett he is no more than one of "them." Rather than her own true love he is her possession—"You're the only person I've got"—and, as such, his status is no different than Cohn's or Mike's: "You've got Mike," he reminds her. Jake says he still loves her, but love is no longer blind. He interrupts her litany of self-pity in an attempt to make her pity others, as he does, and realize the effects of her actions upon them: "It's been damned hard on Mike, having Cohn around and seeing him with you."

Jake tries to teach Brett to control herself, to "go off like a cat," rather than act like a bitch. His many sleepless nights have convinced him that it is as impossible to select which feelings one will entertain as it is to stop feeling altogether. But he has also learned that while one cannot help feeling, he can help showing his feelings and, worse, acting upon them unwisely. Jake does not tell Brett not to feel; rather, he advises her not to act on her feelings: "Don't do it . . . you ought to stop it . . . you oughtn't to do it . . . you don't have to do that." Jake has learned from Romero's example in the bullring that it is possible, although difficult, to control one's actions. This is, after all, what style is about. Rather than merely putting on a good show in public, as Brett and Mike define it, style is a way of life: disciplining and controlling one's self to exercise grace under emotional pressure.

But Brett is having none of it: "I can't help it. I'm a goner now, anyway. Don't you see the difference?" Jake refuses to allow her to abdicate responsibility for herself: "No." He forces her to admit that she is, indeed, making a conscious choice among a number of alternatives, that she is doing not what she must, but what she wants: "I've got to do something," she answers him, then admits, "I've got to do something I really want to do. I've lost my self-respect." Hers is less a problem of compulsion than of selfishness. Finally, she sees this too: "I've always done just what I wanted." "I know." Jake does, indeed, "know," for he has often suffered the consequences of her irresponsible self-indulgence. He does not try to convince her that she is anything but a bitch: "Oh, I do feel such a bitch." "Well."

But while Jake may not support her, he continues to serve her. He gives up his role as conscience and becomes once again her steer:

"What do you want me to do?" Unlike Brett, he often must do what he does not want to do. He cannot stand up to her, cannot interrupt her nor interrupt himself. Jake's own compulsiveness is part of the all-pervasive circularity, futility and repetitiveness that dominate the novel. Like the sun which rises and sets, like Brett, like Mike and Cohn, Jake seems condemned to go around in circles, unable to control himself or his violently self-destructive "steer" impulses. Forced to choose between his *afición,* or obsession, for Brett and his *afición* for the bullfights, he begins paying the bill for having Brett as a friend, attempting to give her "back her self-respect" at the price of his own. The bill comes immediately: Cohn calls him a pimp and knocks him out while Mike feigns unconsciousness to evade helping him, then later cashes in on the last remnants of Jake's friendship with Montoya to borrow a hundred pesetas. His old comrade, Bill, cannot comfort him, first advising him to search for the one drink "that gets it" then turning on him angrily when his suffering proves immune to drink: "Get tight . . . get over your damned depression." The bulls have no compassion for the steer they have wounded, for "old Jake, the human punching bag."

Jake's feelings of loss, despair, estrangement and futility descend upon him with the impact of a crushing blow, as though he has been wounded anew in another war. Or, rather, it is the same wound and the same war, fought this time on the battlefield of the fiesta, a continuation of the wound and war on the Italian front and the earlier injury and battle on the football field of which he is now reminded. As Mark Spilka points out in "The Death of Love in *The Sun Also Rises,*" "the war, the early football game, and the fight with Cohn have this in common: they all involve ugly, senseless, or impersonal forms of violence, in which a man has little chance to set the terms of his own integrity." The kick in the head in America, the blow to the genitals in Italy, and the visceral wounding in Spain are all evidences of the same wound: impotence, whether in sport, love, war or life, a wound simultaneously of the guts, the balls and the head. Jake has been wounded in the ability to take charge, to control and master, to live with that courage, dominance, independence and stamina which for Hemingway is the essence of masculinity, epitomized in the bullfighter's ability to "live his life all the way up" without fear or compromise. Jake's wound is such that he is unable to get it all the way up. He is unable to stand up to life, experience, women, his inner self. Instead, he is passive. He runs from confrontation, backs down from the bulls, trying to "play it along and just not make trouble for people." Where Robert is unable to get started and Brett unable to stop, Jake's own trouble is his inability to finish, to complete or follow through an action, as he is unable to refuse Brett's demands, although he knows they are degrading and destructive.

Now, in Pamplona, Jake feels the same sense of the world's irrevocable alteration, the same inner dislocation and estrangement he felt in the hospital in Milan or walking home from the football game, when "It was all different . . . and it was all new . . . it was all strange. He is suffering from emotional shell shock, from battle fatigue, and wants desperately to withdraw from the field, set down his suitcase and find a "deep hot bath to lie in." But as long as the crowd is around him to demand his service and his solace, he cannot set down his burden. Although injured himself, he continues to respond to their pain with compassion and responsibility. He climbs upstairs to visit the wounded Cohn, forgives him and shakes his hand. He gives Mike his own bottle of wine, opens and pours it for his shaky friend, then later tucks him into bed, comforting him as though he were a child: "You'll sleep, Mike. Don't worry, boy."

But he himself cannot drink, sleep or wash away the consequences, the burden, of this fiesta. Although Brett seems able to bathe away, if only momentarily, her feelings of guilt and disgust, when Jake finds the "deep stone tub," "the water would not run." He is not too drunk to tot up and pay his bill. The celebration continues outside his window but "it did not mean anything." He sees that he has been blind ("Yes . . . I'm blind"), and knows that in some way his view of the world and of himself has changed, that both have come more sharply into focus: "The world . . . was just very clear and bright, and inclined to blur at the edges. The exact nature and effect of the change become clear to him in the peace and solitude of San Sebastian.

Away from Pamplona and the crowd, Jake is reintroduced to the pleasure of his own company. Apart form the brief, exhilarating thrill of the actual bullfights, there was little pleasure for him in the fiesta. Even his joy in liquor had been lost, for he drank too quickly, solely to get drunk and without tasting the wine. Now, removed from the heat and noise, he realizes once again how good life can be when his emotions are under control. "Through with fiestas for a while," he appreciates the unadulterated pleasure of his quiet life: "It was pleasant to be drinking slowly and to be tasting the wine and to be drinking alone."

Unlike Brett, who needs noise, crowds and company, if not an audience, Jake is not afraid of being alone nor does he, like Cohn, spend most of his time looking for ways to run away from himself. He enjoys being by himself, walking, reading, drinking, watching the crowds, listening to music. By himself he experiences regenerative moments of utter quiet—of sleep, relaxation, solitude— which enable him to continue, rising fresh with the sun each morning, no matter what has happened the night before. Unlike Vicente Girones, he was not killed in the rush of bulls at Pamplona. Like Romero, who performs, although battered, or the bicycle racer, who, despite his painful boils, refuses to abandon a race he may win, Jake, although wounded, holds on. Unlike Brett, Mike or Cohn he is able to bear his own pain. He does not create scenes nor does he take out his frustration on others, use them, or attempt to make them pay for his hurt. He has a form of courage and self-control as valid, if not as spectacular, as Romero's: the courage to bear his feelings, the control to "not make trouble for people," a source of strength which is, like Romero's, inherent, not something he acquires, as Cohn learns to box. His inner life, of which he has been so afraid, provides him with strength as well as "trouble." It is turbulent but also abides, like the earth whose freshness he so enjoys; like the sea, whose haunting presence Jake is aware of throughout the novel, it is a source of life and pleasure as well as of "bad weather."

Jake rejects for the moment the simple, "safe, suburban" life of France as he rejects the simple-minded bicycle team manager who pompously announces that "following and organizing the road races had made him know France." Jake wants to face the unknown, "in the destructive element immerse." He decides to confront the sea. Although he appreciates France as "the simplest country to live in" because "everything is on such a clear financial basis," he returns to Spain where "you could not tell about anything." He is not as crippled as he thought and he can handle more than a life based solely on the simple exchange of values. He can get to know himself, can face his own sort of bulls within his own bullring. In San Sebastian he is not content merely to float on top of the calm water, but dives deep beneath the surface, "swimming down to the bottom . . . with my eyes open." He faces his wound and himself, and sees, finally, "how to live in it."

At San Sebastian he confronts his fears. He knows the destructive power of the ocean and his limits as a swimmer. He is a cautious man.

Although "it felt as though you could never sink," the sea will kill him if he gets overtired or overconfident. He tries "to keep in the trough and not have a wave break over me." Climbing up on the raft, away from land and people, he surveys the terrain: "On the other side of the narrow gap that led into the open sea was another high headland. I thought I would like to swim across the bay but I was afraid of cramp." Jake would like to swim in the open sea, become as involved with life, with Brett, with emotions, as bullfighters can, but he is afraid of "cramp," of wounding. He is afraid of drowning in the open sea, of facing the bull head-on rather than vicariously, of a love affair, of women, of his unconscious, of a life without limits. Yet he also sees that there is no shame in facing his fears and limitations squarely, acknowledging them, and living with and within them as best he can. Indeed, there is a kind of courage in such a confrontation and realization. People who refuse to accept their limitations are, in the terms of the novel, either fools, drunks or dead men; they end up committing suicide with the bulls. Although he cannot swim in the open sea, there is still much that he can enjoy: "Then in the quiet water I turned and floated. Floating I saw only the sky and felt the drop and lift of the swells . . . the water was buoyant and cold." Nor does his wound exempt him from the responsibility of living well. Unlike the others, he does not use his limitations as an excuse for self-indulgence and irresponsibility. He realizes that he must live in a limited world, but he also knows that within that world he can live with cleanliness, order and style: "After a while I stood up, gripped with my toes on the edge of the raft as it tipped with my weight, and dove cleanly and deeply, to come up through the lightening water, blew the salt water out of my head, and swam slowly and steadily in to shore."

Although not a bullfighter, a conqueror and destroyer of savage beasts, Jake is more than a taxidermist, a lover and collector of animals already slaughtered. While he does not have Romero's consummate ability to dare, disarm and destroy that which threatens him, he can have a richer life than the count, who in his avid pursuit of the safe and nonthreatening is "dead, that's all." The price of the count's carefully controlled life has been his reduction of other people to commodities, to stuffed dogs, with whom he never really engages, offering money but never himself. Jake, on the other hand, realizes the value of compassion, of giving and sympathizing as well as controlling. He does more than just "not make trouble for people": he responds to them with a compassion, responsibility, understanding and forgiveness that set him apart from the rest of his careless crowd.

But San Sebastian is a place Jake visits; he does not live there. The seashore is a cool and peaceful interlude; in the interior, the war and hell of modern life burn undiminished. Jake's Rest and Recuperation leave is brief. A "military-looking" postman summons him back into the battle, delivering his orders—two telegrams from Brett, with whom Jake has yet to make a separate peace. The old illusion of power and love momentarily reasserts itself, greeted this time with disgust at his role rather than romantic melancholy or self-pity: "Send a girl off with one man. Introduce her to another to go off with him. Now go and bring her back. And sign the wire with love. That was it all right." San Sebastian has been "all shot to hell."

But when he awakens on the train the next morning to see "Madrid come up over the plain," the lessons of San Sebastian are still with him. Madrid is the city at "the end of the line," "the sun-hardened country" where "all trains finish." It's the city where illusions end. In Madrid, Romero has paid the bill for his affair with Brett. Even Brett has faced an unpleasant truth about herself in Madrid: Romero, much younger than herself and ashamed of her, is not her "sort of thing." And in Madrid, this city of renunciation, Jake at last renounces his dreams about Brett. The old games, the old "lines," the old trains of thought, all "finish there. They don't go on anywhere."

On his way to Brett's hotel room, Jake passes "through the gardens, by the empty palace and the unfinished church on the edge of the cliff." He bypasses the relics of the past, the "antiquities" and "suitcases." He leaves behind his old longings for religion (the church) or romance (the gardens) or an external authority (the palace) to order his life, illusions which were in themselves incomplete and desperate ("empty . . . unfinished . . . on the edge of the cliff"). He leaves behind, as well, his dreams of the Garden: "Couldn't we just live together, Brett? Couldn't we just live together? . . . Couldn't we go off in the country for a while?" Instead, Jake gets off in "the high, hot, modern town." He disembarks in hell, but it is a clean, well-lighted hell, one with room to breathe and light to see. The heat that bakes Madrid is the heat of the sun, not the dark, crowded, smoky denseness of the dream-ridden Parisian bals. Madrid is a hell of realization and self-knowledge, Jake's harsh moment of truth. No longer in France, the "easiest, simplest country to live in," Jake has said good-bye to all that, to the easy deceptions and cowardices of his life in Paris. He is in another country, and his illusions, those familiar stuffed animals, are dead.

Jake enters Brett's hotel room neither lover nor knight nor partner in the destructive dream business. He and Brett no longer form a working "we." Instead, he announces himself with "it's me." He sees Brett clearly and with detachment: "The room was in that disorder produced only by those who have always had servants." Brett is, at last, a real and discrete person, not a symbol or token or projection of himself, as she has been. What Jake sees in the disordered bed brushing her short hair is not a "Circe" begrimed in her own wallow or a Siren who has been shorn. He sees no symbols but a suffering human being. He responds to Brett with pity: "She was trembling in my arms. She felt very small." He knows that while she is kissing him, she is "thinking of something else." He knows he has no part in her sufferings. He is not the First Cause of them; she is not miserable for want of him. Her affair with Romero had nothing to do with him; he was only her "servant" to be "utilized" in getting her way. Brett, in her sick and selfish world, makes no distinction between servants and friends. But in her hotel room Jake knows he is no longer her servant, one who is compelled to obey; rather, he is her friend who chooses to comfort her: "Tell me about it." Jake consoles and defends her, agrees with her and supports her, lying for pity's sake: "You were probably damn good for him." When her defensive self-deceptions break down, he holds her shaking and crying in his arms, wanting nothing from her for himself.

However, once Brett's vulnerability has been rearmored by Jake's compassion and a few drinks, she no longer needs his arm to uphold the supportive defense of her illusions, nor his hand to help her swallow them; "her hand was steady enough to lift [the Martini] after that first sip." In the cool bar of the Palace Hotel Brett has found a safe and familiar harbor and no longer clings to Jake as though drowning in the open sea. Then Jake begins reestablishing his distance from her, disengaging himself from her company, refusing to slip back into his old role of steer-confidant-servant, that old "dead end." When Brett boasts that "deciding not to be a bitch" is "sort of what we have instead of God," Jake answers "Some people have God . . . quite a lot," aligning himself not with Brett but with those many others whose lives have meaning, purpose and order ("God"). Jake has within himself what F. Scott Fitzgerald called the "fundamental decencies," honesty, carefulness, endurance, courage, which make him part of the "quite a lot" who "have God." Jake may be himself "the unfinished church on the edge of the cliff." Perhaps his wound is such that he will never finish, never complete nor be completed, like Romero, but he is still "a church."

Jake will be Brett's friend, but he will no longer be her barman, serving with "wonderful gentility" the "coldly beaded" illusions she requires in order to feel "set up" within a cool refuge from the heat and light outside. He will not be as he was in Pamplona, a polite servant who absorbs blame for the carelessness of others ("I should have asked, you know"), perpetuates their illusions ("As they were before?"), and knows when he isn't wanted, going "far enough up the bar so that he would not hear our conversation." Living within her self-absorbed circle, for Brett all cities are the same, but Jake knows he is in Madrid: "You could feel the heat outside through the windows." He knows that although Brett has no friends, there are many eager to be her servant. He knows that for her there is nothing special about him as there is nothing special about this particular barman nor about this particular bar: When Brett exclaims, "Isn't it a nice bar," he contradicts her: "They're all nice bars."

Although Brett is comfortable drinking in the Palace Hotel bar, coming in from San Sebastian Jake has passed by "the empty palace." He gets hungry, too hungry to be satisfied with the "rotten" food the Palace offers: " 'Where will we have lunch?' I asked Brett. . . . 'Here? . . .' 'It's rotten here in the hotel.' " His appetites are too strong to be satisfied with the chilling, romantic concoctions served up by the empty palace; although lethe and nepenthe for Brett, they are hemlock for him. Demanding more substantial nourishment, he takes himself to "one of the best restaurants in the world." Jake does not need to settle for "rotten" food and deadly games. There is a world beyond Brett and the empty Palace bar, a world of appetites he can satisfy, in which there is more and better to sustain him than Brett or the empty palace can provide: "We had roast young suckling pig. . . . I ate a very big meal and drank three bottles of *rioja alta.*" Although Brett "never ate much," Jake's world is rich in sensations: "I like to do a lot of things." He refuses to enumerate or discuss those "things" for Brett; they are a world in which she does not belong, pleasures she does not enjoy.

Brett, feeding off martinis and men, is never satisfied and always ravenous; Jake, satisfying his hunger in more substantial ways, eats, and is fulfilled: "I feel fine." Brett continues to batten upon her illusions, preferring stuffed dog to roast young suckling pig. She is convinced that Jake is getting drunk because they love but cannot have each other, that his suffering is breaking down his self-control. Jake is drinking a great deal but for no reasons she would understand: "How do you know?" Giving up the illusion hurts; it is, indeed, painful to realize not only that he is not loved but that he probably never will be. Yet the pain of starvation and the steady diet of humiliation and shame were more painful still. He sees that he cannot subsist on a dream which has ceased to nourish him, can no longer phantasize that he is full. Malnutrition is another way of committing suicide with the bulls; Jake has realized that, as Brett says, he doesn't "have to."

In telling Brett that he is "not getting drunk," he is telling her that he can control his behavior, that he is no longer compelled by her. He can drink his wine without getting blind. He can enjoy and complete his meal. He can control his behavior and his emotions so that the pleasure of his sensations is undiluted: "I'm just drinking a little wine. I like to drink wine." He cannot control the bulls but he can control himself. He can control the destructive compulsions which ruin his life.

Brett does not get the message for she still hasn't seen Madrid: "I haven't seen Madrid. I should see Madrid." Jake offers to show her the town, but does not run immediately to service her, refusing to interrupt his pleasures to take care of her needs. He finishes his wine first. He takes care of his own appetites; he takes care of himself. When he does enter the taxi, *he* "told the driver where to drive." In control of himself and this situation, he can end his destructive liaison with Brett: " 'I'll finish this,' I said."

He and Brett are still close, still sharing the same war world, still forming their own community. Yet while in the cab in Paris, "our lips were tight together," in Madrid Jake observes that "*Brett* moved close *to* me" but "*we* sat close *against* each other." Jake can feel where he stops and she begins. The community he chooses to form with Brett in Madrid is not the same as they shared in Paris. They no longer feed off the same fantasies and illusions, the same phases and phrases; they are no longer joined at the mouth. Instead, they are two separate people with two separate selves within two separate bodies which touch but never merge.

Brett does not realize the dream is over. She rests "comfortably" within the circle of Jake's arm, within the circle of the hired cab, within the circle of her compulsions, within the circle of her illusions: "Oh, Jake . . . we could have had such a damned good time together."

Jake is not comfortable. Brett is "pressing against" him, the weight not only of her solid physical presence but also of her metaphysical demands. The policeman, the projection of that part of Jake's self capable of arresting his destructive impulses, stops him once again from destroying himself, from "committing suicide with the bulls." Jake has erect and vigorous within him—if not without—a source of masculinity too potent to allow him to be taken for a ride: "He raised his baton. The car slowed suddenly." Responding to Brett with pity and irony, compassion and control, Jake breaks the circle: "Isn't it pretty to think so?"

*T*he Sun Also Rises:
One Debt to Imagism

Linda W. Wagner

Ernest Hemingway's appreciation for Ezra Pound is widely known—his constant praise for Pound during a life marred by broken friendships and bitter words; his 1956 check for $1000, sent to Pound seemingly in lieu of the Nobel Prize medal. Yet Hemingway's fiction is rarely read as having benefited from his intense relationship with the older writer in the early 1920s. We know the legends of the young Hemingway in Paris, apprentice to Stein, Joyce, and Pound, but we have never known what happened to Hemingway's early work. John Peale Bishop remembers, however, that the early manuscripts went to Pound and "came back to him blue penciled, most of the adjectives gone. The comments were unsparing." Whereas Stein's influence was mainly general, it would seem that Pound's dicta were substained with practical suggestions.

By the early 1920s, Pound had enriched his earlier imagist and vorticist theories with precepts directed toward prose. From 1916 to 1918 he had read all of Henry James's writing, in the process of editing the James issue of *The Little Review;* and his long friendship with Ford Madox Ford was finally bearing conscious fruit. So that by the time of his meeting with Hemingway, Pound was deeply interested in prose; in fact, in 1923, he helped William Bird bring out the six books of "new prose" that were to reform prose in the same way Imagism had revitalized poetry a decade before. Among those six books were Wil-

From *The Journal of Narrative Technique* 2, no. 2 (May 1972). © 1972 by Eastern Michigan University Press.

liams's *The Great American Novel,* Pound's *Indiscretions,* and Hemingway's first book, *Three Stories & Ten Poems.*

Pound's excitement over Hemingway's writing (judging it the best prose he had read in forty years) probably allowed the presence of those ten poems in a series dedicated to prose. By 1922, Hemingway had written more poems than stories, poems easily marked as Imagist. Among others, "Along with Youth" and "Oklahoma" illustrate well the chary use of words, the reliance on free verse, and the emphasis on the observable detail of an "Image."

During the years following 1913, when the essays about imagism first appeared, the trademark of that poetic movement was concentration. One of the primary aims was "To use absolutely no word that does not contribute to the presentation," a directive aimed at eliminating from poetry its weak phrases and lines of filler. "Use either no ornament or good ornament," Pound warned; "Don't be descriptive. . . . Go in fear of abstractions." Such axioms demanded that the poet employ his craft consciously, a word at a time, and that he give his impressions the sharp focus of the image.

Pound also defined the image as "that which presents an intellectual and emotional complex in an instant of time." By stressing the wide inclusive powers of the image, he greatly strengthened the imagist concept; and his emphasis on *speed* gave new life to the post-Victorian poem that was nearly buried in expected details. As he continued, "It is the presentation of such a 'complex' instantaneously which gives the sense of sudden liberation . . . that sense of sudden growth which we experience in the presence of the greatest works of art"—epiphany, if you will.

The imagists usually worked in free verse forms because they could thus more easily attain organic form, a shape consistent with the mood and subject of the poem being written. Concentration, speed, and the use of the writer's own conversational language—these were the chief means the Imagists chose to present those objects or experiences which would convey the "white light" of full meaning. Concentration, speed, and the use of the writer's own conversational language—these are certainly trademarks of the famous Hemingway style.

Influence studies are impractical unless intrinsic evidence exists in quantity. The montage effect of the highly compressed stories and vignettes of Hemingway's 1924 *in our time* is the young writer's most obvious tribute to imagism itself, and has been noted by several critics. But perhaps the most sustained example of the imagist method transferred to prose is that maligned novel, *The Sun Also Rises* [*SAR*], 1926. In using the methods of suggestion, compression, and speed within the outlines of traditional novel form, Hemingway achieved a lyric evocation of one segment of life in the 1920's.

Perhaps we should remember that Hemingway was disappointed throughout his life because *SAR* was the novel most often misread; it was the "naturalistic" Hemingway, or at any rate, the "realistic" novel. As he recalled much later, "I sometimes think my style is suggestive rather than direct. The reader must often use his imagination or lose the most subtle part of my thought."

The Sun Also Rises is not, of course, a picture of the "lost generation." Hemingway's poetic method of telling the reader that has caused some confusion. His epigraphs to the book and his final title (the book was called *Fiesta* in its European publication) prove that to him Stein's comment is indeed only "splendid bombast." He uses Stein's comment as the first epigraph for the novel, but the second— the quotation from *Ecclesiastes*—follows it, as if in contradiction:

> One generation passeth away, and another generation cometh; but the earth abideth forever. . . . The sun also ariseth, and the sun goeth down, and hastenth to the place where he arose. . . . All the rivers run into the sea; yet the sea is not full; unto the place from whence the rives come, thither they return again.

By choosing an affirmative phrase as title, Hemingway further reinforces his view, that these characters are not "lost," but merely "beat up." More important, they still have the strength to act against worn-out social forms and find truth for themselves. Jake does, when he gives Brett to Romero in order to make her happy; and Brett does when she sends Romero away. But, because society's arbitrary evaluations of these acts would be unsympathetic, Hemingway has to create the organic whole of the novel so that the acts in themselves convey the proper nobility. It is a difficult task, bucking conventional morality; but Hemingway made it even more difficult by using techniques that could easily be called "poetic," at least in relation to Pound's terminology.

One of the most troublesome of Hemingway's techniques was the strict first person narration. Jake Barnes, with his self-effacing terseness, gives the readers of *SAR* only skeletons of action and characterization. We know very little about Bill and Mike, for example, though everything Hemingway tells us about Bill is positive. But in Mike's scenes, interpreting his remarks is sometimes hard. The same kind of ambivalence surrounds both Brett and Jake. Obviously they are the protagonists, but some of the circumstances surrounding them could stand a more sympathetic explanation—or at least a fuller one— than Jake with his assumed stoicism can realistically give them. Hemingway tried rewriting this novel in third person, so that his 1926 audience would have help with the somewhat unconventional characters, but he evidently liked that effect less well. So he returned to the strictly "objective" presentation of Jake's telling his own story, as it occurred, rather than in a past tense, which would at least have allowed for more reflection. This turning loose a character on an audience, reminiscent as it was of Pirandello, was also a manifestation of Pound's principle, "Direct treatment of the 'thing' concerned," with little ostensible interference from the author. How different Jake Barnes's version of his story was from Carrie Meeber's account of hers.

When Pound directed writers to "Use absolutely no word that does not contribute to the presentation," he was implying a sharp selection of detail. Because Hemingway's selection of detail was so accurate, even skeletal presentations are usually convincing. Brett's bowed head as Mike and Robert argue shows well her tired submission to the present situation, just as Jake's drinking too much after Brett leaves with Romero tells us clearly his emotional state. The repetition of mealtime and drinking scenes in the novel is particularly good for showing the slight but telling changes in a few recurring details. It is of course these changes in the existing relationships that are the real center of the novel, rather than any linear plot.

Following the sometimes minute vacillations in a friendship, or the subtle shadings in a conversation, admittedly demands close attention from the reader. As T. S. Eliot was to point out, reading the modern novel requires concentration as intense as reading poetry—as well as training in that kind of skill. "A prose that is altogether alive demands something that the ordinary novel-reader is not prepared to give."

Hemingway also used a somewhat oblique characterization of his protagonists. Jake and Brett are not always present. Jake as narrator usually speaks about others rather than himself, and when he does think about his own dilemma, it is again in the laconic phrases that leave much to the reader's own empathy. Even though Hemingway introduces Jake in the opening chapter, his focus seemingly falls on Robert Cohn. He tells us innocently enough that Cohn was a college boxing champ, although "he cared nothing for boxing, in fact he disliked it." Then Hemingway begins to accumulate related details; later we see that Romero loves his bullfighting, just as Bill and Jake love fishing. We must then be suspicious of a man who devotes himself to something he dislikes. Subsequent chapters continue the parallel descriptions of Jake and Cohn, and less apparently of Frances Clyne with Brett. It is a stroke of genius that Hemingway waits until we have clearly seen what Jake and Brett are not to present them for what they are—sad but honest people— together, in a would-be love scene.

The Sun Also Rises is also filled with passages that could easily be considered images if they were isolated from their context. An image to Pound was to be more than just a pictorial representation: "an image presents an intellectual and emotional complex in an instant of time." The brief moment when Brett enters the café in the company of homosexuals combines a good set of graphic details with the evocation of Jake's sad excitement and anger as he sees her:

> A crowd of young men, some in jerseys and some in their shirt-sleeves, got out. I could see their hands and newly washed, wavy hair in the light from the door. The police-man standing by the door looked at me and smiled. They came in. As they went in, under the light I saw white hands, wavy hair, white faces, grimacing, gesturing, talking. With them was Brett. She looked very lovely and she was very much with them.
>
> One of them saw Georgette and said: "I do declare. There is an actual harlot. I'm going to dance with her, Lett. You watch me."
>
> The tall dark one, called Lett, said: "Don't you be rash."
>
> The wavy blond one answered: "Don't you worry, dear."
>
> And with them was Brett.

The policeman's smile, the grimacing, the dancing—Hemingway often worked through actions to reveal character and specific mood. But the touchstone here, as often throughout the book, is Jake's own mood, his astonished sadness, caught in the simple refrain line, "And with them was Brett."

Not only does Hemingway use concentrated descriptive passages, he also moves quickly from one passage to another, sometimes without logical transition. This use of juxtaposition to achieve speed in impressions is another poetic technique, enabling a short piece of writing to encompass many disparate meanings. Near the end of the novel, when the reader's attention should be on Brett and Romero as lovers, or on Jake as sacrificial figure, Hemingway instead moves to the account of a young man killed in the morning bull run. "A big horn wound. All for fun. Just for fun," says the surly bartender, picking up one of the repeated key words in the book—*fun, luck, values*. The bartender's emphasis on the unreasoning fun ends with Hemingway's objective report of the younger man's death, his funeral, and the subsequent death of the bull.

> The coffin was loaded into the baggage-car of the train, and the widow and the two children rode, sitting, all three together, in an open third-class railway-carriage. The train started with a jerk, and then ran smoothly, going down grade around the edge of the plateau and out into the fields of grain that blew in the wind on the plain on the way to Tafalla.
>
> The bull who killed Vicente Girones was named Bocanegra, was Number 118 of the bull-breeding establishment of Sanchez Taberno, and was killed by Pedro Romero as the third bull of that same afternoon. His ear was cut by popular acclamation and given to Pedro Romero, who, in turn, gave it to Brett, who wrapped it in a handkerchief belonging to myself, and left both ear and handkerchief, along with a number of Muratti cigarette-stubs, shoved far back in the drawer of the bed-table that stood beside her bed in the Hotel Montoya, in Pamplona.

Hemingway follows this already wide-reaching image with the suggestion of Cohn's "death" as Brett leaves with Romero. This brief descriptive sequence, then, has established the deaths of man, bull, man—all at the whim of the fiesta and its larger-than-life hero, the matador.

Another device used frequently in the book is Hemingway's recreation of natural idiom—in both dialogue and introspective passages—and perhaps more importantly his use of prose rhythms appropriate to the effect of the writing desired. Although the imagist axiom, "Compose in the sequence of the musical phrase, not that of the metronome," was more liberating to poetry than it was to prose, it also spoke for a kind of freedom in prose—sentences unrestricted in tone, diction, or length because of formal English standards. In passages like this opening to part 3, Hemingway arranges sentences of varying lengths and compositions to create the tone he wants (here, a melancholic nostalgia), a tone which may be at odds with the ostensible facts of such a passage.

> In the morning it was all over. The fiesta was finished. I woke about nine o'clock, had a bath, dressed, and went down-stairs. The square was empty and there were no people on the streets. A few children were picking up rocket-sticks in the square. The cafés were just opening and the waiters were carrying out the comfortable white wicker chairs and arranging them around the marble-topped tables in the shade of the arcade. They were sweeping the streets and sprinkling them with a hose.
>
> I sat in one of the wicker chairs and leaned back comfortably. The waiter was in no hurry to come. The white-paper announcements of the unloading of the bulls and the big schedules of special trains were still up on the pillars of the arcade. A waiter wearing a blue apron came out with a bucket of water and a cloth, and commenced to tear down the notices, pulling the paper off in strips and washing and rubbing away the paper that stuck to the stone. The fiesta was over.

In these two paragraphs Hemingway moves from an emphasis on Jake's feelings and actions to the specific details of his locale, using those details to complete his sketch of Jake—alone, and now numbly realizing only that "it was all over." To open the second section with more description of Jake helps the reader keep his focus on the protagonist. The observable details are significant to the story (here and usually throughout the novel) primarily because they help identify an emotional state. Even the movement within this passage, building from the short rhythms of the opening to the longer phrases of the penultimate sentence, and coming back to the restrained "refrain," suggests a crescendo in feeling.

"The fiesta was over," repeated as it is in varying contexts, is an example of Pound's *organ base,* which term he described as "a sort of residue of sound which remains in the ear" and acts to establish mood.

That Hemingway was cognizant of the effects single repeated words or phrases might have is evident not only in his fictional techniques but in his comments about this repetition. Lillian Ross, for one, quotes his saying, "In the first paragraph of *Farewell*, I used the word *and* consciously over and over the way Mr. Johann Sebastian Bach used a note in music when he was emitting counterpoint." It seems unlikely that Hemingway would have missed Pound's later enthusiasms about the "prose tradition in verse." As Pound explained.

> Good writing is writing that is perfectly controlled, the writer says just what he means. He says it with complete clarity and simplicity. He uses the smallest number of words. . . . Also there are various kinds of clarity. There is the clarity of the request: Send me four pounds of ten-penny nails. And there is the syntactical simplicity of the request: Buy me the kind of Rembrandt I like. This last is an utter cryptogram. It presupposes a more complex and intimate understanding of the speaker than most of us ever acquire of anyone. It has as many meanings, almost, as there are persons who might speak it.
>
> It is the almost constant labour of the prose artist to translate this latter kind of clarity into the former; to say "Send me the kind of Rembrandt I like" in the terms of "Send me four pounds of ten-penny nails."
>
> ("The Serious Artist")

Hemingway's emphasis on clarity and seemingly simple diction certainly reflects these kinds of distinctions.

The passage describing the fiesta also provides a good example of Hemingway's failure to use overt symbols (a failure which troubled many critics enough that they began inventing parallels between bulls, steers, and men). In repeating "The fiesta was over," Hemingway suggests broader implications for "fiesta"—a natural expectation of gaiety and freedom, here ironically doomed because of the circumstances of the characters. Through the description, we easily feel Jake's nostalgia, but not because fiesta is a true symbol; it never assumes any existence other than its apparent one. As Pound, again, had phrased the definition, "the natural object is always the adequate symbol . . . if a man use 'symbols' he must use them that their symbolic function does not obtrude." In one sense, in *The Sun Also Rises,* the amount of liquor a person drinks is symbolic—of both the kind of person he is, and the emotional condition he is in. So too is anger, and various stages of it. But the purely literary symbol—which the unsuccessful fireworks exhibition might suggest—is rare. Even the fireworks sequence is used more to show various characters' reaction to the failure than it is to represent another object or state of being *per se*. That Brett does not want to watch the failure is as significant for her character as the fact that she enjoys the artistry of the bullfights.

A corollary to the principle about symbolism is Pound's warning that the writer "Go in fear of abstractions." Love, hate, grief, religion, death, fear—these are the prime movers of the novel, yet the words scarcely appear. *The Sun Also Rises* is essentially a study of various kinds of love, yet no character ever discusses that passion. We are forewarned of Hemingway's definition to come in *Death in the Afternoon,* that "obscenity" is "unsoundness in abstract conversation or, indeed, any other metaphysical tendency in speech." As Floyd Watkins has capably pointed out, Hemingway characters are nearly always to be mistrusted when they speak in abstract terms, whereas Hemingway heroes identify themselves by their preference for the concrete.

Perhaps more than being a study of kinds of love. *The Sun Also Rises* is the paradigm of Jake's initiation into the fullest kind of that emotion. Jake's self-abnegation is not martyrdom; he knows he can not benefit from Brett's affair with Romero. But his education throughout the book consists in learning just how much his love—and hers—can bear. In part 1, it is Jake who wishes they could marry. By part 3 he has learned that any fulfillment of their relationship is impossible. There is no question that he still loves Brett, perhaps even more in her new-found and convincing nobility.

The novel in its three-part division is also the story of Brett's coming to maturity. Although in part 1 she considers herself one with the Count and Jake, the men share satisfactions she does not understand. By the end of the novel she has lost the coy femininity that makes her somewhat cloying. She has thought of someone else— Romero— and she continues thinking, of Mike and—always—of Jake. Stanley Edgar Hyman suggests, "The key action of the book is Brett's renunciation of Romero for the boy's own good, the first truly unselfish act of her life." It could well be that her separation from the church is suggested throughout the novel to help build toward the ending, with her turn to Jake. Brett has no suprahuman comforts; she must call Jake, and the reader must see her telegram to him, as he does, as completely natural.

In the first novel, Hemingway appears to have drawn a little on a
Hamlet-like situation. The many male characters act as either comple-
ments or foils to Jake, and the inevitable comparisons serve to keep
Jake before us at all times, whether he is or not. By making him
physically less than a competitor, however, Hemingway allows Jake *as
person* rather than as male to occupy the center of these relationships,
even the peripheral ones with Krum and Woolsey, the Britisher Harris,
and the Basques. All of these masculine ties help to sustantiate Jake's
real if injured manliness (see Hemingway's *Paris Review* comments),
and add pathos to his love affair with Brett. Jake's wound is his ironic
gift from life, and he has no choice but to live with it—gracefully.
Never again will Hemingway create such a sensational wound for a
protagonist, even in the more obviously war-oriented novels, [but it
does serve a powerfully dramatic function in keeping the otherwise
normal Jake out of the normal rivalry for Brett's affections.]

Yet, for all his anguish, what does Jake say? Hemingway's choice
of idiom for his hero could well have been autobiographical, but it also
bears the trace of Pound's ideal character, who speaks in his own
unliterary voice, speaks in cryptic suggestion, and speaks with truth.
"I've got a rotten headache," when he can no longer bear seeing Brett;
"I wanted to get home." The leave-taking scene with Brett after the
dialogue with Count Mippipopolous has Jake vacillating between "Don't
be sentimental" and then, after a kiss, "You don't have to go." But
after Brett does go, Hemingway gives us some brief introspection so
that we understand the depth of Jake's feelings. When he comes to the
more important good-byes at the end of part 1, as Brett is going to San
Sebastian, Hemingway relies on our earlier knowledge, and gives us
Jake as an objective sketch: "The door opened and I went upstairs and
went to bed." We can presumably re-create the rest for ourselves.

Hemingway relies on Jake's silence or near-silence frequently, not
only in the love scenes. Jake says only "Wasn't the town nice at
night?" trying to reach Cohn through his own foggy bombast. (Jake's
method here is Imagist also, bringing Cohn back to one specific
experience, one night, one town; and having Cohn react like the most
literal-minded of men.) Instead of dialectics, Hemingway here gives us
suggestion.

Even Jake's wound is given in a simple declarative sentence, the
poignancy of its terseness aided by the opening modifier: "Undressing,
I looked at myself in the mirror of the big armoire beside the bed."
The only adjective in the sentence describes a piece of furniture; the

situation itself needs no description. Hemingway is, graphically, and in mirror image, "presenting," as Pound had edicted. The mention of bed also adds pathos to the brief line. The concentration on the furniture offers a moment of deflection also, before Hemingway brings us back to more understatement:

> Undressing, I looked at myself in the mirror of the big armoire beside the bed. That was a typically French way to furnish a room. Practical, too, I suppose. Of all the ways to be wounded. I suppose it was funny.

The climatic act of the novel, for Jake, his giving Brett to Romero, is another model of suggestive gesture instead of speech: "He looked at me. It was a final look to ask if it were understood. It was understood all right."

The chief danger in reading Hemingway is, I think, to overlook this rather apparent origin of many of his stylistic traits. Simplicity has too often become simple-mindedness, just as Williams's "No ideas but in things" has become "No ideas." For instance, a recent essay by Ihab Hassan equates Hemingway's style with the character of Jake Barnes. I agree with Hassan's summary of Hemingway's remarkable tightness in writing, "Its rigor, terseness, and repetitions, its intractable concreteness and vast omissions, resist rhetoric, resist even statement, and discourage the mind from habitual closure." We cannot read Hemingway with any sense of complacence because we are thrown too much on our own, and the old patterns of expectation do not work. But Hassan goes on to move from seeing style, somehow separated, to seeing style as the only possible means of re-creating any Hemingway hero, any Hemingway theme, because he finds Hemingway very close to a contemporary "blankness and rage. . . . Indeed, Hemingway's fiction makes for itself a place in the tradition of silence that extends from Sade, through Kafka, Genet, and Beckett, to the inverted literary imagination of our day." He continues,

> the ethic of Hemingway's characters is not only reductive but also solitary. What they endure, they can never share with others. Existentially, they remain alone; they find momentary communion only in a dangerous ritual. Always they disengage themselves from the complexities of human relations, and simplify their social existence to the primary functions of the body. "The only thing that could spoil a

day was people . . ." Hemingway writes. "People were always the limiters of happiness except for the very few that were as good as spring itself."

While Hassan's thesis in the complete essay is almost convincing, I am bothered by his tendency to overstate— just as Hemingway's use of *always* in the above excerpt is quickly disproved, so can Hassan's be a few lines before. There is a tone of pride here that is misleading; an attitude of "my-knowledge-is-so-dreadful-that-I-cannot-communicate-it." Perhaps the Hemingway protagonist is "alone" in that he is usually limited to a few confidants rather than a menage. But he does have intimates—Bill Gorton, the Count, Montoya, in a sense Romero, and in another sense, Brett. In fact, Jake seems much less isolated than the miserable Cohn, who has literally no one to talk with. And yes, the kind of idiom Hemingway uses is terse and cryptic, but primarily because the emotions are too big to handle in abstract words, not because no emotions exist, or because there is no desire to communicate. *The Sun Also Rises* gives evidence, in its various set scenes, of a great deal of communication. Jake understands perfectly what he must do for Brett, and Brett knows how little she has to say to reach him (in contrast to Frances Clyne who takes an entire chapter to do what Brett can do in three lines). "Let's not talk," Brett tells him. "Talking's all bilge."

The tacit understanding that exists here is better evidence of the author's interest in love, it seems to me, than of his obsession with death. The too-facile equation between death and silence need not shadow every cryptic idiom in American literature. Neither is the prevalent mood in this novel one of terror, as Mr. Hassan later states. (Terror of what? In Jake's eyes, the worst has already happened.) It seems to be rather one of sorrow, of sorrow growing from the unfulfilled love of Jake and Brett which acts in turn as a graphic image for the loves of the many other characters—men with men as well as men with women—which come so seldom to fruition. For those few relationships that had the warmth of the sun in his title, Hemingway was only too grateful. In fact, most of his fiction stands in tribute to just such slight moments.

In his eagerness to present rather than to tell (to render rather than report), Hemingway erred only in following the imagist doctrines perhaps too closely. *The Sun Also Rises* is a difficult book to read correctly, until the reader understands the way it works; then it becomes a masterpiece of concentration, with every detail conveying multiple impressions, and every speech creating both single character and complex interrelationships. It also takes us back to Pound's 1923 description of the best modern prose, which should "tell the truth about *moeurs contemporaines* without fake, melodrama, conventional ending." There is nothing fake about anything in *The Sun Also Rises*, least of all the writing. And to read it as a masterpiece of suggestion makes one compliment Mark Schorer for his statement that Hemingway had in his career written "the very finest prose of our time. And most of it is poetry."

False Dawn:
The Sun Also Rises Manuscript

Michael S. Reynolds

Over a half a century ago, *The Sun Also Rises* was published, metamorphosing Harold Loeb forever into Robert Cohn. Fifty-four years later, we still treat the novel and its characters as if they were our contemporaries, part of that period we still call the Modern Age. In 1926, Hemingway said of Henry James that he was as historical a figure as Byron or Keats and was dead as he would ever be. It is time we took the same attitude toward the twenties. *The Sun Also Rises* is as historical as *The Ambassadors,* and the Modern Age is as dead it will ever be. Memories no longer suffice. The text itself is no longer enough.

The physical description of the manuscript, begun by Professors Mann and Young, is still being completed at the Kennedy Library. My analysis is based primarily on the holograph manuscript which contains thirty-seven loose pages and seven stapled notebooks. I also used three typescript fragments and Hemingway's final typescript which lacks the first ten chapters. The last piece of evidence is an eighth notebook, containing a list of titles and an unpublished foreword for the novel.

With a work of fiction, we always see the title first, but it is not always the writer's working title, nor did it always precede the fiction. On the first page of this manuscript is the working title *Cayetano Ordonez.* Beneath it in quotation marks is "Niño de la Palma," the name under which Ordóñez fought in the bullring. Both names are in

---

From *A Fair Day in the Affections: Literary Essays in Honor of Robert B. White, Jr.* © 1980 by Jack D. Durant and M. Thomas Hester. The Winston Press, 1980.

the same black ink that Hemingway used through most of the first draft. On August 11, with 121 pages written, he shifted briefly to blue ink. About this time he changed the working title to *Fiesta A Novel,* which appears in blue on the covers of all seven notebooks.

On September 27, 1925, six days after he had finished the first draft, he made a list of five alternative titles gathered from Ecclesiastes and Paul's First Epistle to the Corinthians:

> The Sun Also Rises—from the familiar quotation.
> Rivers to the Sea—Eccles. 1:7: "All the rivers run into the sea; yet the sea is not full."
> Two Lie Together—Eccles. 4:11: "Again, if two lie together, then they have heat; but how can one be warm alone."
> A quotation from Eccles. 1:18, with no title indicated: "For in much wisdom is much grief and he that increases knowledge increaseth sorrow."
> The Old Leaven—1 Cor. 5:1–7: "It is reported commonly that there is fornication among you. . . . Know yet not that a little leaven leaveneth the whole lump? Purge out therefore the old leaven, that ye may make a new lump, as ye are unleavened."

Thematically, these titles encompass mutability, permanence, and union, the cost of knowledge, and the wages of fornication. It is misleading to construct an analysis of *The Sun Also Rises* based primarily on the title, for it did not govern the writing of the story. The title came last, just as Hemingway said it did.

There is one other title to which Hemingway gave serious consideration: "The Lost Generation, A Novel." It appears in the eighth notebook immediately following his title list. Beneath it, he wrote what he labeled "Foreword," which was never published. This foreword begins with the Gertrude Stein anecdote about the "lost generation" that was to appear later in *A Moveable Feast.* The setting, however, is not Paris, but the provinces. The young mechanic is excellent rather than incompetent. The punch line is the same. The garage owner says about the generation of mechanics who came out of the war years, "They are all a generation *perdu.*" His mechanics, he explains, have come of age after the war, and are once again competent.

Hemingway comments:

I did not hear this story until after I had written this book. I thought of calling it Fiesta but did not want to use a foreign word. Perdu loses a little something by being translated into lost. There is something much more final about perdu. There is only this then to say that this generation that is lost has nothing to do with any younger generation about whose outcome much literary speculation occurred in times past. This is not a question of what kind of mothers will flappers make or where is bobbed hair leading us. For whatever is going to happen to this generation of which I am a part has already happened.

There will be more entanglements, there will be more complications, there will be successes and failure. There will be many new salvations brought forward. . . . But none of it will matter particularly to this generation because to them the things that are given to people to happen have already happened.

In a letter to Max Perkins a year later, he said that he had not taken the Stein epigraph seriously. He had meant to contrast her splendid bombast against the simple statement of Ecclesiastes. It was in this letter that he instructed Perkins to cut the "vanity of vanities" part from Ecclesiastes: That, he felt, would make his point clearer, which was that the earth abideth forever. He told Perkins he had not meant the book to be a hollow or bitter satire, but a tragedy with the earth abiding as the hero.

His after-the-fact statement of intention has been taken seriously, for there is evidence in the book to support it. Yet, only six days after finishing the first draft, he had almost used the Stein quotation as his title. It is always dangerous to take an author's statement of intent as the whole truth. Hemingway said that he did not run guided tours through his work, and I suspect his letter to Perkins may have been triggered by the reviews of the novel. There is no indication that he considered the Stein quote as "bombast" when he wrote the foreword.

The foreword also makes a comment on Hemingway's relationship with Fitzgerald. The "flappers" and "bobbed hair" refer unmistakeably to the then more established writer. In the first draft, Jake, speaking of his wound, says: "What happened to me is supposed to be funny. Scott Fitzgerald told me once it couldn't be treated except as a humorous subject." In his novel, Hemingway accepted the literary challenge.

By referring in the foreword to Fitzgerald's fictions as "literary speculation" which "occurred in times past," he put Fitzgerald prematurely into the museum. Consciously competing with Fitzgerald, Hemingway had read *The Great Gatsby* just a few months before he began *The Sun Also Rises*. Gatsby was on his mind in April 1926, when he had finished the revised typescript. He wrote a jesting letter to Fitzgerald assuring him that his novel followed the outline of Gatsby, but that it had failed because Hemingway had never lived on Long Island. He said Jake Barnes, like Gatsby, was a Lake Superior salmon fisherman (even though there were no salmon in that lake). The novel is set in Newport, R.I., and its heroine, Sophie Irene Loeb, was sentenced to die in the electric chair at Sing Sing for killing her mother. That part, he told Fitzgerald, he got from Dreiser, but practically everything else in the book was his own or Fitzgerald's. The title, he said, came from Sophie's last words as they turned on the current.

In December of 1926, Hemingway wrote Fitzgerald about the reviews. His tone was once again comical but more biting. The reviewers, he said, could not decide whom he had copied most—Fitzgerald or Michael Arlen. He was grateful to Fitzgerald because he liked him. Besides Arlen was an Armenian whom he did not know and it would be a little premature to be grateful to any Armenian. As a token of his gratitude, Hemingway said he would have Scribner's insert a new subtitle in everything after the eighth printing, which would read:

THE SUN ALSO RISES (LIKE YOUR COCK IF YOU
   HAVE ONE)
A Greater Gatsby
(Written with the friendship of F. Scott Fitzgerald, Prophet
   of the Jazz Age)

Having announced the end of his apprenticeship with Sherwood Anderson in *Torrents of Spring,* Hemingway was serving Fitzgerald notice of a challenge of eminence. The vaguely romantic sentimentality of Nick Carraway was no longer viable. There were no more heroes, only survivors. Fitzgerald's recognition of the challenge entered into his critique of both *The Sun Also Rises* and *A Farewell to Arms*.

Still, Fitzgerald contributed to the final shape of the novel. He was responsible for Hemingway's deleting the opening galleys. He was also responsible for a cut in the dedication. Hemingway intended to dedicate the novel to his son as a "collection of instructive anecdotes." Fitzgerald said no. Hemingway explained that the novel was so obviously not a collection of instructive anecdotes and was such a sad story, not one for a child to read, that he had thought it pleasant to dedicate it in this way, but he would take the advice. The reasons for dedicating it to his son, he said, would be obvious. Hemingway's separation and divorce from Hadley, which took place between first draft and publication, is one of the more obvious reasons. The profits from *The Sun* became Hadley's support money. Hemingway made nothing from the novel.

The holograph manuscript is instructive for what it does not contain. The two epigraphs in the published version appeared only after the draft was finished. The manuscript does not divide the action into three books. Nor does the three-book division appear in Hemingway's typescript. Without access to the galleys, conclusions are tentative. In *A Farewell to Arms,* however, Max Perkins made the five-book division just before the novel went to press. More than likely it was Perkins who divided *The Sun.* There is no indication that Hemingway used the three-part structure of the bullfight as a model for the novel. While the divisions are structurally sound, they do not represent the author's intention while writing the book.

In the holograph there is a confusion of names. In the opening chapter, they are all real: Ernest, Hadley, Duff, Loeb, Pat, Don, Quintana and Niño de la Palma. Not until the second chapter did Hemingway begin to fictionalize the summer of 1925. Hadley disappears. Ernest becomes first Rafael, then Jacob. Duff stays Duff to the very end, changing to Brett in revision. Pat Gutherie appears variously as Pat Campbell, Michael Gordon, and finally Mike Campbell. Harold Loeb becomes Gerald Loeb, Gerald Cohn, Robert Cohn. Niño de la Palma changes to Guerrita. He does not become Pedro Romero until the revision stage. So much has been written on the biographical prototypes that I will not rehash it here. Suffice to say that names were a problem. They continued to be a problem through galley revisions where Hemingway acquiesced to Perkins by dropping reference to Henry James and Joseph Hergesheimer. Hemingway told Perkins that it had been a mistake to put real people in a book, one that he hoped he would never make again.

One point the manuscript makes no clearer is the nature of Jake Barnes's wound. Undergoing few revisions, Jake's condition remained ambiguous from first draft to final copy. The deleted portions of the holograph add nothing. In the George Plimpton interview, Hemingway insisted that Jake was not emasculated in the manner of a steer.

But Hemingway may have been overreacting to Philip Young's analysis of the novel. One phrase, added in the typescript, identifies Jake as a World War I pilot who was wounded while "flying on a joke front like the Italian." The source for Jake's problem may have been a Navy pilot Hemingway had known in the Milan hospital, 1918.

Despite substantial revisions in certain passages and the massive deletions from the opening chapters, the holograph manuscript is remarkably smooth. A large portion of it went straight to print with few, if any, revisions. In *Hemingway's First War,* I have proposed an elaborate scheme of daily recopying to account for the smoothness of the *A Farewell to Arms* manuscript. Hemingway would have been amused. After reading *The Sun*'s holograph, I rejected my earlier explanation. When the young Hemingway was writing well, much of his draft needed no revision. When it went badly, he tended to take out whole paragraphs and whole pages, sometimes as soon as he had written them.

Some of the deleted material was removed not because it was poorly written, but because it seemed irrelevant to the main story. Hemingway, who saved everything, later used some of the Paris material in *A Moveable Feast.* The anecdote of Ford Madox Ford mistaking Aleister Crowley for Hillaire Belloc is the most prominent example. Two other Ford anecdotes were cut, never to reappear.

Hemingway also deleted several passages where Jake tries to explain his relationship with Brett Ashley. As narrator, Jake realizes that the reader may find it difficult to believe their hopelessly unrequited love, or that there can be friendship without fornication. One deleted passage gives more background on Jake's recovery in the British hospital where he met Brett. At two other points he insists that he has made a fine life for himself without women. He realizes that his explanations have not made Brett any more understandable. Finally he says:

> As for how Brett Ashley felt and how things that happened
> to her affected her, I am not a psychologist, I only put down
> what she did and what she said. You will have to figure that
> out by yourselves.

Much of this cut material is laconic, slightly self-pitying, an emotion that Jake, himself, realizes he cannot afford.

In the first draft there is a reference to Turgenev, vestiges of which appear in the novel. In Pamplona when Jake cannot sleep, he reads from *A Sportsman's Sketches*. This reference has not received much attention from critics, but its presence is not accidental. Between October 1925 and January 1926—the period between the completion of the first draft and the beginning of the revised typescript—Hemingway read Turgenev's *Lear of the Steppes, A Sportsman's Sketches, Torrents of Spring, House of Gentle Folk* and *Fathers and Children.* On December 15, 1925, he recommended *Fathers and Children* to Fitzgerald. It was not the best of Turgenev, he said, but it had some swell stuff in it. A writer should learn from everybody who had ever written if they had something to teach. The trouble with most writers was they only learned certain concrete ideas from the classics which were only important as discoveries. If you only got your ideas from other writers, he told Fitzgerald, it was like rediscovering the law of gravity. In a note to himself, he wrote: "Education consists in finding sources obscure enough to imitate so that they will be perfectly safe." Years later he told George Plimpton: "I used to try to write better than certain dead writers of whose value I was certain."

Philip Young has suggested that Hemingway was impressed by Turgenev's brevity, simplicity and intensity. Further study of *The Sun Also Rises* may show that the Russian's influence goes beyond style. Hemingway's crash reading course may have had a deeper purpose. If he was competing with Turgenev, he may have been evaluating his opponent. One suspects that the Russian's influence will be found in Hemingway's tone, attitude and handling of theme. It may be instructive to examine Hemingway's deletions in light of his reading.

Scholars and critics labor under a handicap when they reconstruct an author's purpose, for they are apt to impose their own methods on the author. Hemingway, for example, did not organize his material in the Fitzgerald manner, no matter how much we would like for him to have done so. To suppose that he did in his first two novels is misleading. Hemingway did not plot *The Sun Also Rises* until he was well into the story, and then not carefully.

The opening holograph chapter covers the first day of the Pamplona fiesta. The first nine pages of the second chapter are a false start, giving the background of the principal characters. Crossing out most of it, Hemingway began the revised chapter 2: "To understand what happened in Pamplona you must understand the quarter in Paris." He intended to begin the novel in Pamplona, flash back to Paris, and cycle the action gradually back to the opening day of the fiesta—a traditional *in medias res* structure. His intention held through the entire first draft.

When he had finished what is now the Paris section of the novel, he made a brief outline that he generally followed:

Chapter XIII	finished work Gerald not going
Chapter XIV	ride to Burgette—fishing, return to Pamplona
Chapter XV	Duff, Gerald, and Mike thru the party at the wine shop. Mike's first outburst.
Chapter XVI	Encieno, first corrida brings back to point where book starts; goes on with that night—the South American—the dancing place. Noel Murphy. Count shows up. Gerald fights with Nino.
Chapter XVII	Duff sleeps with Nino.
Chapter XVIII	Corrida. Duff goes off with Nino. Count refuses Mike a job. Bill goes to Paris. Mike talks, goes to Saint Jean de Luz to wait for Duff. Gerald talks, goes to San Sebastian afterwards [to] Paris. I go down into Spain to bring Duff back. Get her letter.

Noel Murphy and Count Mippipopolous did not show up for the fiesta, but the rest is familiar. Like Rinaldi and the priest in *A Farewell to Arms,* the Count is one of Hemingway's fascinating characters who disappears, victim of the unplotted novel.

When Hemingway began his typed revision, he tried three times to open the novel in Pamplona. He tried once in the first-person point of view. Twice he tried shifting into a third-person, but the attempt was stiff and awkward. Each time he broke off the draft after a few pages. Finally he abandoned his opening chapter, beginning the typed draft: "This is a novel about a lady." For the next fifteen pages, he filled in the biography and relationships of Duff, Mike and Jake. On Fitzgerald's advice, Hemingway cut this from the novel in the galley stage. It was not until page sixteen of the typescript that the familiar words appear: "Robert Cohn was once middle weight boxing champion of Princeton."

These same words appear on page forty-nine of the holograph manuscript. Hemingway solved his difficulties with the opening chapter simply by truncating the novel. He did the same thing at the beginning of "Indian Camp," at the end of "Big Two-Hearted River," and at the end of *A Farewell to Arms*. The structural difficulties that critics have had with the novel reflect the difficulties of the author. Had Hemingway followed his original intention, our exegetical interpretations of structure would never have been devised.

If his opening gave him difficulty, the conclusion was right on the money. The printed version ends exactly as the holograph. Only the final line was revised. It began:

"It's nice as hell to think so."
to:
"Isn't it nice to think so."
and finally to:
"Isn't it pretty to think so."

The ending is tight and understated, but it concludes a story that Hemingway did not intend to tell when he began the manuscript. Early in the first notebook there is a deleted authorial comment on structure:

In life people are not conscious of these special moments that novelists build their whole structures on. That is most people are not. That surely has nothing to do with the story but you can not tell until you finish it because none of the significant things are going to have any literary signs marking them. You have to figure them out by yourself.

This scaffolding points directly to Henry James. Carlos Baker has already suggested the main similarities of technique and theme between the two dissimilar writers. I suggest that the inception of *The Sun Also Rises* came from just such a Jamesian "special moment."

That moment is found in the first fourteen pages of the holograph. In the hotel on the first day of the fiesta, Ernest and Quintana discuss the need for protecting the promising young bullfighter from predatory women. Immediately afterwards, Ernest introduces Duff to Niño de la Palma, and Pat tells Niño that the bulls have no balls. While they are drinking, Quintana enters the room:

He started to smile at me when he saw Nino with a big glass of cognac in his hand, sitting laughing, between me and two women, one with bare shoulders and a table full of drinks. He did not even nod. All of a sudden I realized how funny it was.

The scene is familiar for it appears in chapter 16 of the novel. Although he cut the first forty-nine pages of manuscript, Hemingway saved this scene for it was the core of his story. When he revised the passage, he understood that nothing about the scene was funny, and he cut the last line of the paragraph.

Here, finally, is the exciting force that raises the important questions in the novel: Will the woman corrupt the bullfighter? What role will the narrator play in this possible corruption? Traditionally this moment should have occurred early in the novel. It would have had Hemingway stuck to his original plan. To this point in the novel the sustaining question has been: Who will sleep with Brett? The answer has been *everyone*. All that has taken place has been, in effect, the introduction which traditional novelists dispose of in the first chapter. Hemingway knew what he was doing. In a deleted comment he said:

> Probably any amount of this does not seem to have anything to do with the story and perhaps it has not. I am sick of these ones with their clear restrained writing and I am going to try to get in the whole business and to do that there has to be things that seem as though they had nothing to do with it just as in life.

Hemingway is closer to the critical theory of Howells and James than we have suspected. In *The Sun Also Rises,* he was more interested in character development than in plot.

The biographical exegetes have underestimated the importance of Cayetano Ordóñez, the bullfighter, Niño de la Palma. His two names, however, were the first words Hemingway set to paper when he began the draft. The bar scene, which is the germ of the novel, focuses directly on him. I suggest that Hemingway's initial impulse was to write a novel about the corruption of Niño de la Palma, possibly ending with his death or public humiliation.

This hypothesis is supported by substantial internal and external evidence. First, we must realize that Pedro Romero is the idealized bullfighter whose classic style had been long awaited to save the bullring from its decadence. Had Hemingway modeled his matador completely on Niño, he would have told a different story. In *Death in the Afternoon,* he described Niño's disastrous career:

> Cayetano Ordonez, Nino de la Palma, could manage the muleta perfectly with either hand, was a beautiful performer

> with a great artistic and dramatic sense of a faena, but he was
> never the same after he found the bulls carried terms in
> hospital, inevitable, and death, perhaps, in their horns as
> well as five thousand peseta notes between their withers. . . .
> Courage comes such a short distance; from the heart to the
> head; but when it goes no one knows how far away it goes;
> in a hemorrhage, perhaps, or into a woman . . . sometimes
> one woman takes away and another gives it back.

Pedro Romero resembles Niño only in his skills, not in Niño's loss of
courage. Pedro loses courage neither to a woman nor to a wounding,
if we are to believe Brett.

One might argue that when Hemingway wrote the book, he did
not know how badly Niño would fall. But the composition of *The Sun
Also Rises* took place while Ernest and Hadley were following the
bullfights of the post-Pamplona summer. They saw Niño fight more
than once. Shortly after revising the novel, Hemingway wrote an
unpublished feature story that catalogued Niño's failure as he had
observed it during the 1925 season:

> Nino de la Palma who seemed such a beautiful bullfighter de-
> composed altogether when he had a bad bull. . . . if the bull
> did not want to charge he knew no way to make him. There
> is one sovereign way to make a bull charge and that is to get
> close enough to him. But if you approach within a certain
> distance you will be caught absolutely if you do not know
> exactly what the bull will do.   Nino had not learned. . . .
> his nerve went absolutely to pieces. He went through his
> seventy-eight corridas, killed one hundred and fifty-seven
> bulls and was never wounded once. But he did it at the cost
> of panics, scandals, and being protected by the police from
> the crowd. . . . Nino de la Palma was last year's hope for a
> great bullfighter.

What Niño de la Palma proved incapable of doing, Pedro Romero
does perfectly. In the last *corrida,* Romero's first bull will not charge
the cape.

> Romero had to make the bull consent with his body. He had
> to get so close that the bull saw his body, and would start
> for it, and then shift the bull's charge to the flannel and
> finish out the pass in the classic manner.

In contrast to the decadent Belmonte, the only name in the book unchanged, Romero is the classic bullfighter. In changing the name from Niño to Pedro Romero, Hemingway changed the character.

A number of curious holograph passages are cut in the typescript. For example, a slightly misquoted couplet from Marvell's "To His Coy Mistress" appears on a loose page preceding the opening chapter and again on the cover of the fourth notebook:

> The grave's a fine and secret place
> But none I think do there embrace.

As no one in the novel goes to his grave, one wonders why Hemingway retained the quote as a possible epigraph almost to the galley stage. If the novel had focused on the corruption and death of the bullfighter, such an epigraph would have been both ironic and appropriate.

In the first version of chapter 2, there is a long anecdote about death which focuses finally on Niño. The narrator tells how there were certain things his mother would rather see him in his grave than do. As a young boy at his uncle's funeral, he discovered the meaning of "in his grave," and the shock of recognition was permanent: "It seemed strange that anything I could do would make her wish to see me in that condition and it prejudiced me against all her views and moral values." He continued, bringing the point of the anecdote home:

> So I will not judge the gang who were at Pamplona and I will not say that it would be better for Nino de la Palma to be in his grave than to train with a crowd like that because if he did train with them he would be in his grave soon enough and no matter how attractive a grave may seem to old people or to heroes or as an alternative to sin to religious mothers it is no place for nineteen year old kids.

This emphasis on death makes sense only if one of the characters in the novel were to die. In the sixth notebook, by which time Niño's name had been changed to Guerrita, a seemingly gratuitous aside is cut: "This is not a story about bull fighting. There is not any big final bull fight scene. Guerrita does not get killed. Nobody gets killed." Cancelling these lines as soon as he wrote them, Hemingway then relates the final corrida, including a detailed description of Guerrita's two bulls. The assurance that the bullfighter was not going to die was, perhaps, a vestige of the story he had intended to write.

Eliminated, along with the Paris background, is an early passage which bears on the problem:

> Now you can see. I looked as though I were trying to get to be the hero of this story. But that is all wrong. Gerald Cohn is the hero. When I bring myself in it is only to clear up something. Or maybe Duff is the hero or Nino de la Palma. He never really had a chance to be the hero. Or maybe there is not any hero at all. Maybe a story is better without any hero.

Niño could not be the hero. He never had a chance because he could not sustain his performance. To perform well once is not enough. A hero must be able to do it well each time he goes into the ring, even under the worst circumstances. Hemingway knew that Niño de la Palma was incapable of sustained excellence. To replace him, he created Pedro Romero, who sustains his performance well under pressure.

By the time the first draft circled back to Pamplona, Niño de la Palma's name had been changed to Guerrita. In a passage deleted from the fifth notebook, Jake says: "The story is Guerrita. For a time Guerrita is the hero. Mr. Gerald Cohn is not the hero. He was the hero for a time but he has been chopped."

Rafael Guerra, who fought under the name Guerrita, was a well-known torero whose first professional appearance was on September 27, 1887. Although he was alive in 1925, Guerrita had retired from the bullring. Hemingway had never seen him fight. In *Death in the Afternoon,* Hemingway wrote:

> When in the accounts we come to Guerrita, another golden-age hero, who corresponds to the period just before, during and after the Spanish-American war you read that the bulls were small and young again; . . . finally Guerrita retires and every one is relieved; they have had enough of him, although once the great Guerrita is gone bullfighting is in a profound depression.

The name Guerrita is used throughout the final three notebooks of the first draft. It does not become Pedro Romero until Hemingway's revised typescript.

Romero was an even more historical figure than Guerrita. In *Death in the Afternoon,* Hemingway said:

> According to historians Pedro Romero, who was a matador
> in Spain at the time of the American revolution, killed five
> thousand six hundred bulls recibiendo between the years
> 1771 and 1779 and lived to die in bed at the age of ninety-
> five. If this is true we live in a very decadent time indeed
> when it is an event to see a matador even attempt to receive
> a bull.

Hemingway associates the slightly decadent Guerrita with the Spanish-
American War, a slightly decadent war. Pedro Romero, the purist, is
linked with the American Revolution. These political associations do
not appear in the novel, but the decline and corruption of the bullfight
becomes a metaphor describing our time. Belmonte, who was once
great but decadent, comes out of retirement with only his decadence
and his contempt for the crowd. At the bullfights, we can see what a
falling off has occurred because we have Pedro Romero for comparison. He becomes the standard of measurement that Niño de la Palma
was not.

Hemingway changed all of the names from his first draft. That he
changed Niño's is not in itself significant. But by changing his name to
progressively more historical, more classical, and less corrupt bullfighters, Hemingway also changed the moral fiber of his character.
The extent of this change can be measured in a deleted scene from the
opening pages of the first draft. In Pamplona, Ernest is awakened:

> At six our door was banged open and three men came in
> carrying a fourth, his legs hanging. I woke as the door
> opened and my first thought was that I must have overslept
> and missed the morning amateur fight and someone was
> being brought in wounded. Then one of the men said, "It's
> not here," and they went out. As they turned I couldn't see
> the face of the man they were carrying. But it looked like it
> was Nino. Anyway they put him in Number Eight.

Although most of the opening chapter was recycled in the typescript,
this scene was eliminated, for it carries the seeds of Niño's corruption,
which Hemingway had decided not to portray.

Pedro Romero becomes the only idealized figure in the novel, but
he is still not the central character, nor is he the hero, as Hemingway
emphasized in his deleted asides and in his correspondence with Perkins. After the fact, he suggested that the earth was the abiding hero of

the novel, but it is not the Spanish earth that is clearly in focus at the novel's end—it is Jake Barnes and Brett Ashley. In his other fiction from the period, Hemingway always left his readers looking directly at his central concern without always telling them what they were seeing. It took readers several years to read some of his stories properly, to understand what had been left out.

Buried in the first draft of the Burguete section there is an exemplum of this principle. After fishing Jake relaxes by reading a collection of A. E. W. Mason mystery stories. All we are told in the printed version is:

> I was reading a wonderful story about a man who had been frozen in the Alps and then fallen into a glacier and disappeared, and his bride was going to wait twenty-four years exactly for his body to come out of the moraine, while her true love waited too, and they were still waiting when Bill came up.

In the holograph there is a two-page synopsis of the story, some of which appears to be direct quotations. Recovering the frozen husband, the wife's lover chips the ice away from his still youthful face. As the wife watches:

> The airs of heaven beat upon Mark Frobisher, and suddenly his face seemed to quiver and his features to be obscured. Stella uttered a scream of terror, and covered her face with her hands. Just as you thought. But there was something else. While he crumbled a small trifle tinkled on the ice with a metallic sound. I read on about the trifle. The trifle was the point of the whole story.

Even in the holograph Hemingway does not say that the "trifle" was the bullet that had killed the husband twenty-four years earlier. What the wife had thought an accident had been a murder committed by her lover. "The trifle was the point of the whole story."

One might argue that Hemingway cut this passage as being extraneous. But why didn't he cut the entire reference? I suggest that by leaving out even more than Mason left out, Hemingway illustrates his principle of underplaying the most important point of his story. In *Death in the Afternoon* he told us: "If a writer of prose knows enough about what he is writing about he may omit things that he knows and the reader, if the writer is writing truly enough, will have a feeling of those things as strongly as though the writer had stated them." In "Ten Indians," written immediately after the first draft of *The Sun,* Hemingway does not need to tell us that Nick has had sexual relations with the Indian girl. What is left out of *The Sun Also Rises* is the loss that Jake Barnes suffers.

Critics have long been aware that Jake is the only real loser in the novel. The other wanderers exit no worse off than they began. Brett's self-congratulatory chatter at the end does not deceive either the reader or Jake. She may not have completely corrupted the bullfighter, but she has not been saved by her charity. Jake asks her not to talk about it, not because he admires her action, but because he does not want to think about what happened in Pamplona. He knows he can never go back. By pimping for Brett, he has cancelled his membership in the select club of aficionados. Montoya may have once forgiven his drunken friends, but he will never forgive him for assisting in Pedro Romero's corruption. The novel's most understated passage occurs when Jake pays his hotel bill. He tells us: "Montoya did not come near us." This, the cruelest line in the book, goes without comment. Here is the "trifle" dropping on the ice. Jake, who started with so few assets, now has even fewer to get him through the night. If the novel "is such a hell of a sad story," as Hemingway said it was, the sadness resides in Jake's loss.

Hemingway's initial intention was to describe the corruption of a promising bullfighter. The novel he wrote is the corruption of Jake Barnes. In that "special moment" in the hotel dining room, both stories are implicit.

What's Funny in *The Sun Also Rises*

James Hinkle

> *"Hemingway, why do you always come here drunk?"*
> *"I don't know, Miss Stein, unless it's to see you."*
> Quoted in JOHN ATKINS,
The Art of Ernest Hemingway

> *"Oh, it was a joke then."*
> *"Yes. To laugh at."*
> *The Sun Also Rises*

Readers have come up with many reasons for admiring *The Sun Also Rises* [*SAR*] but no one, so far as I know, has made much of the jokes in the novel. The free-associating banter of Bill Gorton, the fractured English of Count Mippipopolous, occasional sardonic comments by the narrator, Jake Barnes, have of course been noted. But jokes in *SAR*? What jokes? Most readers seem to find the book no funnier than did Harold Loeb, prototype of *SAR*'s humorless Robert Cohn: "I do not remember that Hem was much of a spoofer as a young man. Perhaps he developed a taste for it as age overtook him." The prototype of Bill Gorton, Donald Ogden Stewart, a professional humorist himself, said flatly that "written humor was not his [Hemingway's] dish."

Yet I propose to point to about sixty submerged jokes in *SAR*—if by "jokes" I can be understood to mean all of the various kinds of plays on words whose effect is incongruous or funny once they are recognized. Few of them will make anyone roll in the aisle, but they have their moments. My aim is not to defend Hemingway's sense of humor or to sort his jokes into categories. My aim is simply to identify

From *The Hemingway Review* 4, no. 2 (Spring 1985). © 1985 by Ohio Northern University.

his jokes—to demonstrate by example that there are many more of them in *SAR* than we have realized. Playing with the multiple meanings inherent in words is a pervasive feature of Hemingway's writing.

Most readers have approached Hemingway with serious expectations, and these expectations have determined pretty much and limited what they have found. But Hemingway always claimed to be at least a part-time humorist. He is consistently unsympathetic to those who looked down on him when he himself "committed levity":

> [L]ots of criticism is written by characters who are very academic and think it is a sign you are worthless if you make jokes or kid or even clown.

> The bastards don't want you to joke because it disturbs their categories.

> "Joke people and you make enemies. That's what I always say."

Anyone who has read through Hemingway's letters must have been struck by his persistent reliance on humor. Even when he is most serious he often develops his argument in an ironic or flippant or mocking tone. We know from his letters that he thought the first draft of *SAR* was funny. *The Torrents of Spring,* clearly intended as a funny performance, he wrote between finishing the *SAR* first draft and before starting the revision. And in an inscribed copy of the printed *SAR* Hemingway called the novel a "little treatise on promiscuity including a Few Jokes."

I want to present my sixty *SAR* jokes roughly in order of their difficulty, moving from relatively obvious examples to more subtle or ingenious or likely-to-be-overlooked ones. Begin with a simple pun whose effect is mild humor:

> Everything is on such a clear financial basis in France . . . If you want people to like you you have only to spend a little money. I spent a little money and the waiter liked me. He appreciated my valuable qualities.

But that is not a typical *SAR* pun, because it calls attention to itself. Most of Hemingway's puns are less insistent:

> Brett was radiant . . . The sun was out and the day was bright.

That should be a clear example. Here is another:

> For six months I never slept with the electric light off. That
> was another bright idea.

Sometimes a pun is introduced and then played with:

> The publishers had praised his [Cohn's] novel pretty highly
> and it rather went to his head.

Where else except up would high praise go? This is followed on the
next page by adding "steep" to the pun on "high":

> Playing for higher stakes than he could afford in some rather
> steep bridge games.

Another example:

> In the dark I could not see his face very well.
> "Well," I said, "see you in the morning."

That is a variation of:

> There is no reason why because it is dark you should look at
> things differently from when it is light. The hell there isn't!

The narrator, Jake Barnes, is not the only one in the book who is
alive to puns. On the evening Bill Gorton arrives in Paris Jake asks
him:

> "What'll we do to-night?"
> "Doesn't make any difference. Only let's not get daunted.
> Suppose they got any hard-boiled eggs here?"

"Hard-boiled" eggs to guard against becoming daunted. The meaning
of "hard-boiled" we already know from Jake:

> It is awfully easy to be hard-boiled about everything in the
> daytime, but at night it is another thing.

Sometimes the pun depends on the reader knowing at least something of a foreign language. After Cohn and Jake have their first
near-fight:

> We walked up to the Café de la Paix and had coffee.

At least one *SAR* pun is based on a catchphrase of the day. When
Jake leaves Cohn at the end of the first chapter he says:

"I'll see you to-morrow at the courts."

He means the tennis courts, but his sentence is a play on "See you in court."

Sometimes *SAR*'s words make a statement that is literally true in more ways than the presumably intended one. While the effect of these second meanings is usually funny, that is not always the case. Consider the scene when Jake learns from Brett that it was Robert Cohn she had gone to San Sebastian with:

> "Who did you think I went down to San Sebastian with?"
> "Congratulations," I said . . .
> We walked along and turned a corner.

Their relationship at that moment did indeed turn a corner. Jake can't keep back his bitterness after Brett explains that she rather thought the experience would be good for Cohn:

> "You might take up social service."
> "Don't be nasty."

Shortly after Jake has helped set up Brett with Romero, Cohn comes looking for her:

> "Where's Brett?" he asked.
> "I don't know."
> "She was with you."
> "She must have gone to bed."

Yes, that is exactly where she is—in bed, with Romero.

When Brett and Jake approach the Café Select after reaching a romantic impasse in a Paris cab:

> On the Boulevard Raspail, with the lights of Montparnasse in sight, Brett said: "Would you mind very much if I asked you to do something?"
> "Don't be silly."
> "Kiss me just once before we get there."
> When the taxi stopped I got out and paid.

That last is quite a line. Literally it means that Jake gives the taxi driver five or ten francs. But it also means that Jake has an emotional price to pay for his hour in the cab close to Brett. He leaves the Select shortly afterward, walks to his apartment alone, thinks of his wound and of Brett, and then cries himself to sleep.

Mike sees that Brett has a new hat:

"Where did you get that hat?"
"Chap bought it for me. Don't you like it?"

Doesn't he like what? The hat or the idea that a man bought it for her? The first is probably what Brett intended but the second has more meaning for the novel.

Brett makes a remark to Romero that the reader can (and probably should) take in more than one way:

"The bulls are my best friends. . . ."
"You kill your friends?" she asked.
"Always," he said in English, and laughed. "So they
don't kill me." He looked at her across the table.
"You know English well."

There are three meanings in Brett's last comment: first, she could be simply complimenting Romero on his ability to speak English; second, she could be saying that his sure manner, his way of looking at her, show that he knows very well how to make himself attractive to an English lady; third, and more ominous she could be saying that he knows English people very well if he realizes that English friends could kill him. This last meaning is supported by several other passages: Mike says it was his friends, false friends, that did him in. Montoya says about Romero: "Any foreigner can flatter him. They start this Grand Hotel business, and in one year they're through." Jake has already told us that "any foreigner was an Englishman," and Brett says in Madrid after she had sent Romero away, "I'd have lived with him if I hadn't seen it was bad for him," and she hopes it is true when she says "I don't think I hurt him any."

Religion is put in its place by one brief comment:

That afternoon was the big religious procession. San Fermin
was translated from one church to another . . .
"Isn't that the procession?" Mike asked.
"Nada," some one said. "It's nothing."

Jake goes to confession several times in Pamplona. Brett would like to go with him but Jake tells her:

Not only was it impossible but it was not as interesting as it
sounded, and, besides, it would be in a language she did not
know.

Jake's minor joke here is that his confession would not be likely to interest Brett because he does not have any sexual items to report. A more significant meaning concerns the language Brett would not understand. Confessions in a Spanish church would be in Spanish. But in the following sentence we learn that Brett has her fortune told at a gypsy camp, and that too would be in Spanish, and there is no mention then of her not being able to understand what was said. Nor does she have any trouble understanding and being understood by Romero, or the other Spanish men who use her as an image to dance around or to sing to in their hard Spanish voices. The point seems to be that it is the language of the church that Brett doesn't know and it makes no difference whether one takes that to be Spanish or Latin. As she says herself, "I'm damn bad for a religious atmosphere. I've the wrong type of face."

At the end of the book Brett suggests that the satisfaction resulting from decent behavior might substitute for the consolation of religion. Jake is not so sure, so he gently proposes a painkiller more in line with her temperament:

> "You know it makes one feel rather good deciding not to be a bitch. . . . It's sort of what we have instead of God."
> "Some people have God," I said. "Quite a lot."
> "He never worked very well with me."
> "Should we have another Martini?"

Mike obviously has reached the same conclusion concerning Brett:

> "These bull-fights are hell on one," Brett said. "I'm limp as a rag."
> "Oh, you'll get a drink," Mike said.

The most frequent kind of joke in *SAR* is the peculiarly literal one that results when someone (the narrator or one of the other characters) understands (or pretends to understand) a word in a different sense (usually a more literal one) than might reasonably have been expected. This pattern is easier illustrated than described. *The Snows of Kilimanjaro* has a pure example:

> "I don't see why that had to happen to your leg. What have we done to have that happen to us?"
> "I suppose what I did was to forget to put iodine on it when I first scratched it. Then I didn't pay any attention to

it because I never infect. Then, later, when it got bad, it was probably using that weak carbolic solution when the other antiseptics ran out that paralyzed the minute blood vessels and started the gangrene." He looked at her, "What else?"

"I don't mean that."

Frank O'Connor tells a story of an evening when he was James Joyce's guest:

[I] touched the frame of a picture on the wall.

"What's this?"

"Cork."

"Yes, I see it's Cork. I was born there. But what's the frame?"

"Cork."

Some time later, in conversation with Yeats, [I] told him about the picture and its frame. Yeats sat up straight.

"That is mania. That is insanity."

Mania it may be, but it is also funny.

Words deliberately taken as words are the basis of much of the humor in *SAR*. The simplest form of this basic joke in *SAR* can be seen when Jake tries to get by difficult moments with Brett by responding literally to her words rather than to their intended meaning:

"Don't look like that, darling."

"How do you want me to look?"

"What did you say that for?"

"I don't know. What would you like me to say?"

"Darling, don't let's talk a lot of rot."

"All right. Talk about anything you like."

"I was in school in Paris, then. Think of that."

"Anything you want me to think about it?"

Sometimes the literal joke is buried in a seemingly innocent remark. After Cohn knocks Jake out, Jake reluctantly goes to Cohn's room and finds Cohn feeling sorry for himself:

"Now everything's gone. Everything."

"Well," I said, "so long. I've got to go."

and:

> "You were the only friend I had. . . ."
> "Well," I said, "so long."

One time Cohn drops by Jake's Paris office and wants to talk. When it becomes apparent Cohn isn't going to leave, Jake invites him downstairs for a drink:

> "Aren't you working?"
> "No," I said.

Literally that is an accurate response. Jake isn't working; he is at the moment talking with Cohn. But he wants to work and is maneuvering to get rid of Cohn so he can get back to work.

"Hell" is the subject of several instances of unexpected literalness. In one, Jake has just told Cohn that Brett is a drunk and is going to marry Mike Campbell:

> "I don't believe it." . . .
> "You asked me what I knew about Brett Ashley."
> "I didn't ask you to insult her."
> "Oh, go to hell."
> He stood up from the table his face white, and stood there white and angry behind the little plates of hors d'oeuvres.
> "Sit down," I said. "Don't be a fool."
> "You've got to take that back."
> "Oh, cut out the prep-school stuff."
> "Take it back."
> "Sure. Anything. I never heard of Brett Ashley. How's that?"
> "No. Not that. About me going to hell."
> "Oh, don't go to hell," I said. "Stick around. We're just starting lunch."

Jake suggests the crowded condition of hell when he is talking with Cohn about going to South America:

> "Well, why don't you start off?"
> "Frances."
> "Well," I said, "take her with you."
> "She wouldn't like it. That isn't the sort of thing she likes. She likes a lot of people around."
> "Tell her to go to hell."

An interesting use of hell occurs after Jake has helped set up Brett with Romero and then Cohn comes looking for her:

> "Tell me where Brett is."
> "I'll not tell you a damn thing."
> "You know where she is."
> "If I did I wouldn't tell you."
> "Oh, go to hell, Cohn," Mike called from the table. "Brett's gone off with the bull-fighter chap. They're on their honeymoon."
> "You shut up."
> "Oh, go to hell!" Mike said languidly.
> "Is that where she is?" Cohn turned to me.
> "Go to hell!"
> "She was with you. Is that where she is?"
> "Go to hell!"

It is hard to say whether Cohn's "Is that where she is?" refers primarily to "honeymoon" or "hell"—if the two are not indeed the same thing, for when Jake gets to Madrid to rescue Brett from her "honeymoon" she reports: "I've had such a hell of a time," and earlier she had said about being in love: "I think it's hell on earth."

Sometimes someone (usually Jake) deliberately and perversely misunderstands what is said to him:

> "Would you like to go to South America, Jake?"
> "No."
> "Why not?"
> "I don't know. . . . You can see all the South Americans you want in Paris anyway."
> "They're not the real South Americans."
> "They look awfully real to me."

Sometimes Jake deliberately misunderstands but doesn't expect his off-center response to be picked up. Romero is asking about Mike:

> "What does the drunken one do?"
> "Nothing."
> "Is that why he drinks?"
> "No. He's waiting to marry this lady."

Sometimes someone misunderstands unintentionally:

> "You never come here any more, Monsieur Barnes,"
> Madame Lecomte said.
> "Too many compatriots."
> "Come at lunch-time. It's not crowded then."

Jake's objection, of course, is not to the number of customers at the
restaurant but to the fact that most of them are American tourists.

Sometimes the twisting of meaning is intended by the speaker to
be recognized as a joke. Mike tries it:

> "How did you go bankrupt?" Bill asked.
> "Two ways," Mike said. "Gradually and then suddenly."

and Brett:

> "Here come the gentry," Bill said.
> They were crossing the street. . . .
> "Hello, gents!" said Brett.

and Bill:

> "Well," I said, "the saloon must go."
> "You're right there, old classmate," Bill said. "The sa-
> loon must go, and I will take it with me."

and Jake:

> I found Bill up in his room. He was shaving. . . .
> "How did you happen to know this fellow, anyway?"
> "Don't rub it in."
> Bill looked around, half-shaved, and then went on talking
> into the mirror while he lathered his face.

It would be easy to read right over that passage without realizing that
Jake has made a small joke with "Don't rub it in" and that Bill, by
interrupting his lathering and turning around, acknowledges that he
understands it.

Sometimes the joke is in a seemingly innocent throwaway line
that goes along with a conversation:

> "I can't stand it any more."
> He lay there on the bed.

> "All my life I've wanted to go on a trip like that," Cohn
> said. He sat down . . . "But I can't get started."

> "Don't just sit there . . . Don't sit there looking like a
> bloody funeral." . . .
> "Shut up," Cohn said. He stood up.

> "I'm just low, and when I'm low I talk like a fool."
> I sat up, leaned over, found my shoes beside the bed and
> put them on. I stood up.

This last example tells us quite a bit about Jake. Only to a person with
an enormous regard for words would it ever occur to think of standing
up as a remedy for feeling low.

Sometimes words trigger a bizarre train of thought. A waiter asks:

> "Shrimps?"
> "Is Cohn gone?" Brett asked.

Sometimes an expression is acted out:

> "Ask her if she's got any jam," Bill said. "Be ironical
> with her."
> "Have you got any jam?"
> "That's not ironical." . . .
> The girl brought in a glass dish of raspberry jam . . .
> "Poor," said Bill. "Very poor. You can't do it."

Bill and the waitress in different ways give Jake the raspberry.

Brett comes to Jake's room and wakes him up at half-past four in
the morning. Jake makes drinks and listens while Brett talks on about
her evening with Count Mippipopolous: "Offered me ten thousand
dollars to go to Biarritz with him . . . Told him I knew too many
people in Biarritz." Brett laughs but Jake doesn't.

> "I say, you are slow on the up-take," she said. I had only
> sipped my brandy and soda. I took a long drink.
> "That's better. Very funny."

Jake's taking a long drink is not simply a clever response to Brett's
saying he is "slow on the uptake." It is also his way of indicating he
had understood when Brett on the previous page by taking a drink had
acted out one meaning for "one of us":

> "The count? Oh, rather. He's quite one of us."
> "Is he a count?"
> "Here's how." . . . She sipped at her glass.

Occasionally a passage needs to be read aloud for us to realize what is funny. Brett first appears in the book at a *bal musette* with a group of flamboyant male homosexuals. We recognize them by how they talk when they see Georgette:

> "I do declare. There is an actual harlot. I'm going to dance with her, Lett. You watch me."
> The tall dark one, called Lett, said: "Don't you be rash."
> The wavy blond one answered: "Don't you worry, dear."
> And with them was Brett.

Hemingway and Jake do not care for homosexuals. Jake walks away. When he returns to the *bal* Mrs. Braddocks brings up a young man and introduces him as Robert Prentiss. If we continue reading aloud we discover that Prentiss too much have been part of Brett's entourage:

> He was from New York by way of Chicago, and was a rising new novelist. He had some sort of an English accent. I asked him to have a drink.
> "Thanks so much," he said. "I've just had one."
> "Have another."
> "Thanks, I will then." . . . "You're from Kansas City, they tell me," he said.
> "Yes."
> "Do you find Paris amusing?"
> "Yes."
> "Really?" . . .
> "For God's sake," I said, "yes. Don't you?"
> "Oh, how charmingly you get angry," he said. "I wish I had that faculty."

When Jake hears that last speech, he gets up and walks away again. Mrs. Braddocks follows:

> "Don't be cross with Robert," she said. "He's still only a child, you know."
> "I wasn't cross," I said. "I just thought perhaps I was going to throw up."

Robert Cohn wants to be a writer, but listen to his first words in the book:

> "For God's sake, why did you say that about that girl in Strasbourg for?"

Can anyone who can say a sentence like that ever become a decent writer?

Sometimes in order to see what is funny the reader has to do more than read aloud: he has to follow up on implied instructions. Consider this passage taken from Jake's and Bill's first morning at Burguete:

> As I went down-stairs I heard Bill singing, "Irony and Pity. When you're feeling . . . Oh, Give them Irony and Give them Pity. Oh, give them Irony. When they're feeling . . . Just a little irony. Just a little pity . . ." He kept on singing until he came down-stairs. The tune was: "The Bells are Ringing for Me and my Gal."

There is nothing funny here when we simply read the words, although we do quickly figure out what the rhyme word for "pity" is—the word that caused Maxwell Perkins to insist on three spaced periods. But see what happens if we try to sing Bill's words to the tune of "For me and My Gal." We discover there is no way Bill's words can be made to fit that tune. This tell us that Bill must be splendidly rhythm-deaf, and this leads us to understand funny meanings for several other passages—when the Spaniard beats time on Bill's back while trying to teach him a song and Jake comments that Bill "wasn't getting it," and what it must have sounded like when Bill plays the piano to keep warm at the inn at Burguete. As the old advertising slogan put it: "They laughed when I sat down at the piano, but then I started to play."

Some of Hemingway's jokes are like syllogisms with the middle term unstated and which the reader must use his ingenuity to supply. Jake takes the train at Irun and "after forty minutes and eight tunnels I was at San Sebastian." Surely "forty" and "eight" are meant to suggest the wartime forty and eight military transport cars (forty hommes/eight chevaux) and represent Jake's comment on the primitive Spanish rail accommodations of the 1920s. This *has* to be Hemingway's purpose in the passage, for the manuscript of *The Sun Also Rises* shows "forty minutes and six tunnels" and Hemingway later changed it to forty and eight.

One of Hemingway's funniest and most obscure jokes is in Bill's comment about Robert Cohn's telegram to Burguete:

> The telegram was in Spanish: "Vengo Jueves Cohn."
> I handed it to Bill.
> "What does the word Cohn mean?" he asked.

Bill is just learning Spanish. Among the first phrases one picks up in any language (after "yes," "no," "where is," and "how much") is "I come." So Bill presumably has gotten far enough in Spanish to understand "Vengo." But "Jueves" (Spanish for "Thursday") he apparently hasn't learned yet and the appearance of the word gives him no help. "Jueves" is J-U-E-V-E-S. What does that look like or suggest to an American who doesn't know Spanish? Jew. And thus Bill's comment: Why add Cohn? His point is that the message already says "I come, Jew." What other Jews does Cohn think we might be expecting? —This joke is no doubt objectionable in the 1980s but in the 1920s it was one of the ways the game was played.

We recognize Mike's less than rigorous thinking when he says:

> "I gave Brett what for, you know. I said if she would go about with Jews and bull-fighters and such people, she must expect trouble."

Jews and bullfighters and such people? What kind of category is that? I suppose he means people who are not "one of us," but it would be hard to imagine a more vague way of defining that group.

When Jake takes the prostitute Georgette to join his literary friends for coffee after dinner, he introduces her as his "fiancée, Mademoiselle Georgette Leblanc." This is Jake's attempt at a mild joke. The girl is obviously a prostitute, his friends know he has no fiancée, and Georgette Leblanc was the name of a well-known real person—the ex-mistress of Maeterlinck, an actress, singer, and past-middle-aged eccentric who regularly bicycled around Paris in a flowing medieval robe of gold-flowered velvet. The men at the table go along with Jake's joke and all stand up. But Mrs. Braddocks, "a Canadian [with] all their easy social graces" (Hemingway didn't think much of Canada and Canadians), understands nothing of what is happening. She takes Jake's introduction seriously and talks "cordially" with Georgette. When it finally gets through to her that Jake's introduction is not entirely accurate, she calls down the table to her husband to report what she considers an amusing discrepancy: "Did you hear that, Henry? Mr. Barnes introduced his fiancée as Mademoiselle Leblanc, and her name is actually Hobin." At which point Braddocks makes his joke—for the benefit of the others at the table. Proud of his innocent wife and secure in knowing she will not see anything amiss in his saying he knows a prostitute, he says: "Of course, darling. Mademoiselle Hobin. I've known her for a very long time."

Brett's jokes are usually more worldly. Count Mippipopolous drives to the far side of Paris to bring back a basket of champagne for Brett and Jake:

> "I think you'll find that's very good wine," he said. "I know we don't get much of a chance to judge good wine in the States now, but I got this from a friend of mine that's in the business."
>
> "Oh, you always have some one in the trade," Brett said.
>
> "This fellow raises the grapes. He's got thousands of acres of them."
>
> "What's his name?" asked Brett. "Veuve Cliquot?"
>
> "No," said the count. "Mumms. He's a baron."

There are two jokes here—one intended by Brett and a second possible only for Jake and Hemingway. Brett knows the count is interested in women, since he had already offered her ten thousand dollars to go with him to Biarritz or Cannes or Monte Carlo. So when he says he has a friend in the champagne business Brett adds up what she knows and makes her joke: "What's his name? Veuve Cliquot?" Her guess has a kind of oblique logic, since "Veuve Clicquot" is the name of one of France's four great champagnes. Her point is that "Veuve Clicquot" *means* something in French that seems to her to fit the situation—"the widow Clicquot." In fact Veuve Clicquot champagne is called in British slang "the merry widow." Thus, if the count says he knows a champagne grower, Brett is suggesting it would probably be the merry widow. Hemingway's joke is that Brett simply picked the wrong brand. The count actually *does* know one of the great French champagne producers— Baron Mumm.

Earlier in the book Brett makes a joke that Hemingway specifically identifies as joke, but readers seem not to have bothered to try to make sense of it. Jake and Brett are sitting in a taxi at night, moodily discussing how Jake's wound had made impossible what might have been a satisfying relationship. Brett says:

> "When I think of the hell I've put chaps through. I'm paying for it all now."
>
> "Don't talk like a fool," I said. "Besides, what happened to me is supposed to be funny. I never think about it."
>
> "Oh, no. I'll lay you don't."
>
> "Well, let's shut up about it."

"I laughed about it too, myself, once. A friend of my brother's came home that way from Mons. It seemed like a hell of a joke. Chaps never know anything, do they?"

What seemed like a hell of a joke? Answer: Not just to be wounded in the groin but to be wounded in the groin at Mons. Mons was, of course, a major battlefield of World War I, but "mons" is also the "mons veneris" which, as anyone who has had a high-school course in sex education knows, is the polite term for a woman's pubic mound. For a man to have an encounter at "mons" and come away with damaged sexual apparatus does indeed act out the ancient female threat of "vagina dentata"—vagina with teeth. As Brett says, "It seemed like a hell of a joke."

Mike shouts drunkenly to Jake: "Tell him [Romero] Brett is dying to know how he can get into those pants." "Pipe down," someone says. Yes, pipe down. If Joyce in *Ulysses* can make a joke out of "U-P up," Hemingway in *SAR* can explain to anyone who doesn't already know that bullfighters fit into their tight pants "pipe down."

Near the beginning of the book Jake watches a red and green stop-and-go traffic signal. At the end he sees a traffic policeman raise his baton, forcing the cab Jake is riding in with Brett to a sudden halt. Between these two scenes we find a number of references to people waving things—the drummer waving his drumsticks, Bill waving a chicken drumstick, Marshal Ney waving his sword, "the inventor of the semaphore engaged in doing the same." All seem to prepare us for the policeman's raised baton of the final page. It would be hard to imagine a more explicit symbolic acting out of a reminder of the reason Jake cannot satisfy Brett.

I am not the first, of course, to have noticed the sexual overtones of the policeman's raised baton, but I am not aware that anyone has spelled out how the details of the scene work. The baton is a twelve-inch white club. When not being used—when it is at rest—it dangles from the policeman's waist. The policeman is a "mounted" policeman. "Mounted" is itself a sexual word. Presumably here it means that he is riding a horse—thus in the saddle, an easy rider—and this takes us back to Bill's "puts a man on her horse" which is in turn based on "puts lead in your pencil." The policeman is wearing khaki. That suggests a military uniform and is a reminder of the reason Jake cannot now go ahead. But khaki (rhymes with "tacky") is a relatively recent and specifically American pronounciation. In the 1920s in Europe it was "cock-ee" which has an unavoidable sexual suggestion. And to this that a few minutes earlier Jake had trouble entering Brett's hotel because he could not make "the elevator" work, and then he was told that the personages of her establishment were "rigidly selected." The policeman's raised baton forces Jake to confront the fact that he will never qualify for admission to Brett, since "making the elevator work" and a selection process involving "rigid" represent for him impossible requirements.

Jake's jokes (and thus Hemingway's in *SAR*) are all in the ironic mode—variations on Bill's "Give them Irony and Give them Pity." Surely, taken together, and at the very least, the jokes represent one possible and reasonably effective defensive stance for someone who has been wounded in a rotten way on a joke front—which, less literally, seems to have been the situation of almost all young men and women of feeling after World War I.

Toreo: The Moral Axis of *The Sun Also Rises*

Allen Josephs

"Let the others come to America who did not know that they had come too late. Our people had seen it at its best and fought for it when it was well worth fighting for. Now I would go somewhere else." Alfred Kazin cites this passage from *Green Hills of Africa* as an epigraph for the chapter on Hemingway in his new book *An American Procession.* Hemingway, he tells us, "at every stage of his life . . . found himself a frontier appropriate to his fresh needs as a sportsman and his ceremonial needs as a writer." And Hemingway differed from other "American writer-wanderers," such as Melville and Twain, because "Hemingway for the most part chose where he wanted to go." I have started with the same passage to point out the same things but also to point out Hemingway's dissatisfaction with what was happening in America, much of which, in his view, had been "spoiled." Earlier in the same passage Hemingway wrote, "Our people went to America because that was the place for them to go then. It had been a good country and we had made a bloody mess of it."

In the long section which John Dos Passos got Hemingway to cut from the last chapter of *Death in the Afternoon,* Hemingway explained his peculiar odyssey in terms of the three peninsulas—Michigan, Italy, and Spain—he had loved, lived in, and written about. He had loved Michigan very much when as a boy he had spent summers there, but

From *The Hemingway Review* 6, no. 1 (Fall 1986). © 1986 by Ohio Northern University.

each time he returned he found it changed more and more. The forests were cut and the streams were ruined and the fishing was no longer any good. Roads had been built everywhere, the tourists had caught all the fish and the farms had been abandoned. He cared about parts of northern Italy the way he had cared about northern Michigan, and he thought that when Michigan was ruined he could go to Italy as a solution to the problem. It was a matter of finding new good country in an old country. But Italy had been ruined too and made impossible by a tyranny he would not accept. So, via Paris he came to Spain where he liked the bullfights and the people and where he found some things being practiced he believed in.

Hemingway's correspondence from 1923 to 1925 makes it clear that he considered Spain a new "frontier," that is, that he found it still unspoiled. His letters show that he transferred his psychic allegiance from Michigan, via Italy, to Spain. "Spain is the very best country of all. It's unspoiled and unbelievably tough and wonderful," he wrote to James Gamble in December 1923. "There is swell fishing. Like the Black when we first hit it," he told his old fishing buddy Howell Jenkins in 1924. Pamplona was the "greatest country you ever saw and right on the edge of the only trout fishing that hasn't been ruined by motor cars or railroads. . . . The people have any people in the world skinned. . . . You can only live once, Carper, and this is as good as the best of the best days we ever had on the Black and Sturgeon. . . . But Spain is the only country left that hasn't been shot to pieces. They treat you like shit in Italy now. All post war fascists, bad food and hysterics. Spain is the real old stuff."

Fishing, of course, was only part of the attraction. After his first trip to Pamplona in 1923, he sent a long letter to his old roommate and fellow veteran, William D. Horne, claiming that he had "just got back from the best week I have ever had since the Section. . . . You'd be crazy about a really good bullfight, Bill. It isn't just brutal like they always told us. It's a great tragedy—and the most beautiful thing I've ever seen and takes more guts and skill and guts than anything possibly could." In the letter to Howell Jenkins about how great Spain was, he reiterated his enthusiasm: "Honest to Gawd Carper there never is anything like it anywhere in the world. Bull fighting is the best damn stuff in the world." The *toreros* themselves were exactly the kind of people he had been looking for, as he wrote to Edward J. O'Brien: "Do you remember me talking one night . . . about the necessity for finding some people that by their actual physical conduct gave you a real feeling of admiration like the sealers, and the men off the banks [Georges Bank] up in your country [Boston]? Well I have got ahold of it in bullfighting. Jesus Christ yes." Toreros were the most admirable artists of all, he told Ezra Pound: "The Plaza is the only remaining place where valor and art can combine for success. In all the other arts the more meazly and shitty the guy, i.e. Joyce, the greater the success in his art. There is absolutely no comparison in art between Joyce and Maera—Maera by a mile. In a letter to Scott Fitzgerald, written from Burguete in 1925—he had just been fishing in "wonderful country" and was headed for Pamplona and the fiesta he could fictionalize in *The Sun Also Rises*—he made his ultimate pronouncement on the whole subject: "To me heaven would be a big bull ring with me holding two barrera seats and a trout stream outside that no one else was allowed to fish in." Thirty-five years later Hemingway would describe Spain—in the second sentence of *The Dangerous Summer*—as the "country that I loved more than any other except my own." For the young Hemingway it was a matter of the last good country, to transfer the title of a Michigan story to Spain. And at the heart of that country were two of the things he loved best—unspoiled fishing and *toreo,* which, Hemingway's use of the term notwithstanding, we somewhat erroneously call bullfighting.

Trout fishing and toreo, of course, figure prominently in *The Sun Also Rises,* as well. In a long, rambling, discarded section of "Big Two-Hearted River," published posthumously as "On Writing," Hemingway revealed through his most autobiographical character, Nick Adams, the extent to which both these activities concerned him. Nick's feeling about fishing was explicit: "All the love went into fishing and the summer. He had loved it more than anything." But for Nick, just as for Hemingway, toreo would later become paramount: "His whole inner life had been bullfights all one year. . . . Maera was the greatest man he'd ever known."

In an article on *Death in the Afternoon* in the *Hemingway Review,* I have attempted to explain how the "explanation and exaltation of the pristine savagery of the *plaza de toros.* was tantamount to Hemingway's embracing an ancient mystery and iconoclastically rejecting much of what passed for modern Western values." Now I want to explore how and why toreo lies at the heart of *The Sun Also Rises.* In order to do so, we need to keep in mind something Hemingway wrote to Maxwell Perkins shortly after the book's publication:

> The point of the book to me was that the earth abideth
> forever—having a great deal of fondness and admiration for
> the earth and not a hell of a lot for my generation and caring
> little about Vanities. . . . I didn't mean the book to be a
> hollow or bitter satire but a damn tragedy with the earth
> abiding forever as the hero.

I can think of no classic of modern literature that has had as many
and as varying interpretations as *The Sun Also Rises*. Comedy, tragedy,
even Divine Comedy. Jake Barnes as the Fisher King of the Wasteland.
Jake Barnes as a *cabestro,* as a steer, that is, as a gelding. Jake as the
matador. Brett as a *vaquilla,* a fighting cow. Brett as a, yes, symbolic
toro. Brett as an alcoholic nymphomaniac, as the bull-goddess, as the
fertility goddess, and as her modern avatar, the bitch-goddess. The
corrida as a Punch and Judy show; Jake as Don Quixote; Cohn as Don
Quixote; Romero as Don Quixote; Jake as Sancho Panza. And this is
only the tip of the iceberg.

Many of the critical problems derive from an improper or forced
interpretation of the meaning of the *corrida de toros*—the bullfight. It is
perhaps not surprising, then, to find that one of the best interpretations
comes not from a book of literary criticism but from a critical book on
the bulls, John McCormick's erudite study *The Complete Aficionado*.

McCormick makes a number of good points about this novel he
judges "a masterpiece in small that might be considered as the only
war novel in which no shot is fired but the rocket setting off the fiesta
of San Fermín at Pamplona." All the "sympathetic characters have
either been in the war or are toreros. Their shared experience has given
them a common view, a common set of clues, and even a private
language. Cohn . . . is outside the charmed circle."

McCormick has also understood that *The Sun Also Rises* is a novel
of manners: "Although morality as such is almost never on the surface
of the page, conduct, whether moral or immoral, is Hemingway's
exclusive subject. The moral problems of an immoral world occupy
his fullest attention." And he was the first (1967) to understand how we
were supposed to grasp this exclusive—but elusive—subject: "We know
this not from the moralizing of either writer or characters but through
the symbolical burden placed upon toreo. The fiesta at Pamplona
occupies the center of the novel, just as the characters' response to
toreo is a measure of their human value in the eyes of Jake Barnes."
The war and toreo as shared experience, the moral nature of the novel,

toreo as the moral measure of these characters—McCormick's views, with no quixotic attempts to equate *The Sun Also Rises* and previous masterpieces, form the necessary foundation for what follows.

In a quite different vein, H. R. Stoneback has taken a very careful critical look at the geography of *The Sun Also Rises,* much of which, as Stoneback has demonstrated, Hemingway rearranged to suit his own purposes. In Stoneback's reading, the novel becomes a "quest, the pilgrimage undertaken in order to grow in grace." Glossing Bill and Jake's walk through Paris and explaining the significance of the places they pass, Stoneback explores the figurative and symbolic journey they make, a journey which begins "in the shadow of Notre Dame, on the Ile Saint Louis, with its suggestions of the great crusading king and saint," along the rue Saint-Jacques which is not at all in actual fact the "rigid north and south" that Jake proclaims, past the Val de Grace and through the "Port Royal district with its many associations with Pascal, another 'wounded' quester." What does Hemingway intend with this "paysage moralisé"? In Stoneback's words, it was

> the crucial historical importance of the rue Saint-Jacques as the road which led south on the long pilgrimage to Santiago de Compostela, in northwestern Spain. Santiago was well known to Hemingway and for someone aware of the importance of this historical highway as a pilgrimage route, it might indeed seem symbolically, a "rigid north and south."

Stoneback goes on to explain much more about religious allusions and purposely rearranged geography in *The Sun Also Rises,* and he demonstrates quite convincingly the spiritual nature of Jake's quest "to know the 'values' " through the "careful practice of ritual and discipline" and, indeed, the spiritual design of the entire novel. Calling for "a moratorium on the old, weary circular discussions of the 'code,' " Stoneback concludes that "the deepest thrust of this novel is radically spiritual, and it is addressed directly to the radically 'secular age' . . . which has seemed for the most part incapable of deep engagement with Hemingway's vision."

I have quoted Stoneback's article at some length for two reasons: one, because I think it is the most important article to date on *The Sun Also Rises*; and, two, because his decisive groundwork obviates any necessity on my part to prove the "radically spiritual" nature of the work. Citing what is surely the most important passage in *Death in the Afternoon,* in which Hemingway equates the ecstasy produced by a great matador's work with religious ecstasy, Stoneback affirms that in *The Sun Also Rises*

> the bullfight is meant to convey an emblem of moral behavior. For conduct to be moral, then, it must be rooted in courage, honor, passion, and it must exhibit grace under pressure. . . . Measured by these rigorous standards, the behavior of every important character except perhaps Romero is found wanting.

Both McCormick and Stoneback agree—the former on a secular plane, the latter on a more spiritual one—that toreo is the measure of all the characters in the novel.

A significant change in the name Hemingway gave his matador bears out Stoneback's more spiritual interpretation. When Hemingway gave the characters fictional names, Antonio Guerra, "Guerrita," was the name he chose for his young artist, a name which echoed the name of the great nineteenth-century matador, Rafael Guerra, "Guerrita." *Guerra,* of course, means war and the diminutive sobriquet, the nom de guerre as it were, "Guerrita," has the effect of "warrior." When Hemingway rewrote the novel in Austria in the winter of 1926, however, he changed "Guerrita" to Pedro Romero, the name of the eighteenth-century matador who was almost indisputably the greatest of all time. He also rewrote the description of Romero's killing his second bull, changing the method of killing from the usual method to the far more difficult and dangerous way of killing *recibiendo,* or receiving the bull's charge, a method of which the historical Romero was the unchallenged master. The effect of these changes, which I will discuss in more detail later, is to remove the suggestion of war and to enhance the stature and artistry of Romero's work precisely at the climax of the novel.

Notice, please, that I said Romero's *work*, not Romero. And let us remember that both McCormick and Stoneback pinpoint toreo—the bullfight, rather than the bullfighter—as the measure of the men and women in this book. In a passage in the original manuscript, which was titled *Fiesta,* Hemingway wrote that for a while "Guerrita" was the hero. Then he cut the passage. Earlier on he had written that perhaps the matador was the hero of the story. Then he added, "He never really had a chance to be the hero. Or maybe there is not any hero at all. Maybe a story is better without any hero." This passage originally ended chapter 5, and although Hemingway later cut it too, it probably revealed his original intention. In any case, it is toreo itself, the *art* of toreo, that is at the core of *The Sun Also Rises*.

To be sure, Romero creates that art, but a close look at the language Hemingway uses shows us that the work, and "it," is what matters: "Romero's *bullfighting* gave real emotion, because he kept the absolute purity of line. . . . Romero had the *old thing,*" (my emphasis throughout). "The crowd felt *it,* even the people from Biarritz, even the American ambassador saw *it,* finally." "Pedro Romero had the *greatness*. He loved bull-fighting. . . . Never once did he look up. He made *it* stronger that way, and did *it* for himself, too, as well as for her . . . he did *it* for himself inside, and *it* strengthened him. . . . He gained by *it* all through the afternoon." "Each thing he did with this bull wiped [the fight with Cohn] out a little cleaner." The artistic performance at the center of the plaza de toros is not merely the center of attention, it is also the source of moral amelioration and physical antidote.

As Romero's work, his *faena* with his second bull, continues, it becomes clear that he is achieving the kind of great performance that Hemingway would equate with religious ecstasy in *Death in the Afternoon*: "the crowd made him go on. They did not want the bull killed yet, they did not want it to be over. Romero went on. It was like a course in bull-fighting. All the passes linked up, all completed, all slow, templed and smooth. . . . And each pass as it reached the summit gave you a sudden ache inside. The crowd did not want it ever to be finished." Although Hemingway's technical descriptions of the bulls were not yet at their peak in 1925–26, he was obviously trying to describe, to quote the description from *Death in the Afternoon,* the faena "that takes a man out of himself and makes him feel immortal while it is proceeding," that is capable of "moving all the people in the ring together and increasing in emotional intensity as it proceeds . . . in a growing ecstasy of ordered, formal, passionate, increasing disregard for death."

This moral, spiritual, even ecstatic dimension of toreo ought not surprise us, especially if we bear in mind Stoneback's injunction to desist from seeking heros and codes and to concentrate instead on the spiritual. The art of toreo is at the center of *The Sun Also Rises* precisely because it is spiritual. In taurine circles great young performers are not entirely facetiously known as Messiahs. Hemingway used that very term—"Messiah" as well as "Resurrexit"—in his original draft of the novel, and he attempted to describe the effect of great art in the plaza, the great art of "Guerrita"/Romero, by comparing it to the consummation of a first love together with the feeling of death, a combination which returns us to ecstasy. It is probably just as well he cut that passage, too, but the attempt, however overly romanticized, again reveals explicitly the effect he was after.

All the characters who make the pilgrimage to the fiesta at Pamplona are measured—morally or spiritually— around the axis of the art of toreo. Romero, the creator of that art, because he is an innocent and a creator in the face of punishment and death, comes closest to perfection. Montoya and the true aficionados are the keepers of the faith. The morally undiscerning American ambassador and company are splendid examples, by contrast, of what Alfred Kazin meant when he wrote that Hemingway "knew that, morally, the bourgeois world was helpless." They do not know the values, especially not the value of toreo. As Montoya, whom Hemingway once called "a highly moral hotel keeper," puts it: "People take a boy like that. They don't know what he's *worth*. They don't know what he *means*" (my emphasis). Jake knows perhaps better than anyone, even though he betrays him, and Brett, in her finest moment, comes to understand. Cohn, on the other hand, understands nothing and worries that the corrida may bore him. Loveless lover of Brett, vanquished victor of Romero, Cohn is devoid of moral content, a moral bankrupt who is completely out of place at the fiesta, outside, in McCormick's phrase, the charmed circle.

Jake understands better than anyone because only Jake moves freely and knowingly in both the profane world of the Lost Generation and the sacred world of toreo. The very reason for the fiesta is, of course, to stop profane time, clock time, historical time. Jake understands perfectly: "The things that happened could only have happened during a fiesta. Everything became quite unreal finally and it seemed as though nothing could have any consequences." A fiesta is time out of time, sacred time, original time, primal time, *illud tempus* to use Mircea Eliade's term. In fact, the "rituals or important acts" which Eliade lists in *The Myth of the Eternal Return* as abolishing profane time—"alimentation, generation, ceremonies, hunting, fishing, war, work"—read virtually like a catalog of Hemingway's only subjects: eating and drinking; love and sex; hunting and fishing; war; writing; and ritual ceremonies, of which toreo is a clearly supreme example. On the following page Eliade continues as though he were writing on toreo in *The Sun Also Rises*: "Insofar as he repeats the archetypal sacrifice, the sacrificer, in full ceremonial action, abandons the profane world of mortals and introduces himself into the divine world of the immortals."

I have no doubt that Hemingway had a full intuitive understanding of what he was doing with toreo at the center of his novel. In a letter to Max Perkins in 1926 he called toreo "the one thing that has, with the exception of the ritual of the church, come down to us intact from the old days." Toreo is not just the moral axis of *The Sun Also Rises,* it is the *axis mundi* of Hemingway's artistic vision, and it is not accidental that the rituals of the plaza de toros and of the church are joined in Hemingway's mind as they are in much of Spanish art.

In order to see how Hemingway went about sacralizing the fiesta with Romero's great faena and kill recibiendo, how he constantly pared away the trivial and the profane, we need only to compare sections of the original manuscript of the novel in the Kennedy Library with the published text, concentrating on the fictional changes he made in the morally central character of Pedro Romero. Sixty years ago in Schruns, Hemingway did the "most difficult job of rewriting I have ever done . . . in the winter of 1925 and 1926, when I had to take the first draft of *The Sun Also Rises* which I had written in one sprint of six weeks, and make it into a novel." Interesting phrase that last one: "and make it into a novel." But anyone who reads that rough draft he completed in six weeks alongside the published version will understand precisely how Hemingway went about converting an often journalistic and autobiographical account, especially at the beginning, into a classic of modern literature that in the intervening sixty years has lost none of its fascination.

When Hemingway began writing the novel in Madrid and in Valencia in the second half of July, 1925, within days of the actual events that had inspired it, he used real names. It began *in medias res* in Pamplona:

> Cayetano Ordonez
> "Nino de la Palma"
> Fiesta
> I saw him for the first time in his room in the Hotel
> Quintana in Pamplona.

The characters are called Hem, Don, Duff, Pat, Hadley, Harold or Loeb, Quintana, and Nino. What started as a more or less factual account began to evolve into a more fictional account as he continued to write the first draft, and, of course, changed radically in the rewriting as he began to "make it into a novel."

Even though he originally based the characters in part on real people, "inventing from experience," as he often called it, the final creation transcended altogether the historical facts of the summer of 1925. As Hemingway somewhat overstated the case to Max Perkins, "the only stuff in the book that was not imaginary" was the "Brett biography," which of course he cut out at Fitzgerald's urging.

That being the case, what are we to make of this statement from *The Dangerous Summer?*

> I had known Cayetano years before and had written a portrait of him and an account of his fighting in *The Sun Also Rises.* Everything that is in the bull ring in that book is as it was and how he fought. All the incidents outside the ring are made up and imagined. He always knew this and never made any protests about the book.

What concerns me most are the phrases "a portrait of him" and "Everything that is in the bull ring in that book is as it was and how he fought." Those statements need to be taken with a grain of salt since Hemingway transformed Cayetano Ordóñez, "Niño de la Palma," as much or more than he did anyone else, within the plaza de toros as well as without. Hemingway's facts about Spain are frequently not correct, but the myths that he makes from the shards of history are far more satisfying than any accurate reconstruction. "Everything that is in the bull ring in that book" is not as it was, and Pedro Romero is, fortunately, not a portrait of Cayetano Ordóñez. To watch the transformation from Cayetano Ordóñez, who fought as "Niño de la Palma," the kid from the Palm (the Palm was the name of Ordóñez's father's shoe shop which failed), into Antonio Guerra, "Guerrita," and finally into Pedro Romero is to begin to understand how Hemingway turned the base metal of banal facts into *The Sun Also Rises.*

In the in medias res beginning, which was later moved to its chronological position in chapter 15, the matador is called "Nino de la Palma" and then just "Nino." "Cayetano Ordóñez" is never used after the first line of the rough draft. It was as though Hemingway had started with and then immediately abandoned the real man, choosing to use fictionally only the artistic persona, "Nino de la Palma." In fact his matador and Cayetano Ordóñez were nothing alike. Cayetano was called "gay, impulsive and warmly generous" by his admirers, but his detractors spoke of him as a hard drinker, a womanizer, and a spendthrift, in short the classic Andalusian *señorito* who thrived, for a while, on all-night flamenco parties (his wife, Consuelo, whom he married in 1927, was a half-gypsy flamenco dancer). His admirers said he lost his *afición,* his desire to fight bulls, but his detractors claimed he lost his nerve. Hemingway went on at length about Cayetano Ordóñez's cowardice in *Death in the Afternoon,* calling it, among other things, "cowardice in its least attractive form," and he described his season of 1926, as "the most shameful season any matador had ever had up until that year in bullfighting. What had happened was that the horn wound, the first real goring, had taken all his valor. He never got it back." It was not actually Cayetano's first goring, nor was it the worst season a bullfighter had ever had. Still, Hemingway's judgment was somewhat justified after having watched Cayetano be disastrously bad four times running in Pamplona in 1926, so bad that he had failed to kill one of his bulls and had had to be protected from the crowd by the police and later smuggled ignominiously out of the Hotel Quintana's back door to escape on the train.

In 1925, however, he "looked like the messiah who had come to save bullfighting if ever any one did," as Hemingway put it in *Death in the Afternoon.* In the in medias res beginning the narrator and Quintana agree that "Niño" was the best they had ever seen, with the finest and purest style and the greatest authority in the plaza, a description which echoed contemporary accounts of "Niño de la Palma" that year. When Hemingway again turned his attention to the Pamplona section, now in its proper chronological place, he kept the name "Niño de la Palma" and "Niño" through the description of the first corrida. Then he went back and changed the matador's name to "Guerrita," and added a passage about "Guerrita's" background. Hereafter in the rough draft the matador is called Antonio Guerra, "Guerrita," and "Niño de la Palma" has disappeared.

The real matador, that is, has disappeared altogether and a fictional one named "Guerrita" has taken his place. "Guerrita" is—as the real Cayetano Ordóñez was—from Ronda, and his name—as Cayetano's had—echoes that of a great nineteenth-century matador. As Hemingway would explain some years later in *Death in the Afternoon,* Cayetano Ordóñez had the same name as a matador from Madrid famous a hundred years before, Cayetano Sanz; and he was from Ronda, the cradle of the art. In what became one of the most famous phrases in the annals of the bulls, the critic, Gregorio Corrochano, wrote, "Es de Ronda y se llama Cayetano," (He is from Ronda and is named Cayetano), making "Niño de la Palma" famous at once, a kind of instant myth, the newest messiah come to save the corrida. Hemingway tried to use this bit of propagandistic mythmaking for his own purposes to make his fictional "Guerrita" into a "messiah" and also to try to suggest a kind of mythic greatness about him by giving him the same name as the late nineteenth-century master from Córdoba, Rafael Guerra, who, as we have seen, was also called "Guerrita." All of Spain, the narrator in the rough draft tells us, was with him for two reasons: he had the same name as one of the greatest matadors of all time; and he was from Ronda which was the birthplace of the art. With the creation of Antonio Guerra, "Guerrita," we are yet another step removed from the historical Cayetano Ordóñez.

The final steps in the evolution from the historical Cayetano Ordóñez to the fictional Pedro Romero occurred in the major rewriting in Schruns the next winter. Now he had become simply Pedro Romero, dedicated, serious, and dignified; and the messianic propaganda and the too pointed partial coincidences in names, and the *apodos,* the artistic names, such as "Niño de la Palma" or "Guerrita" were cut.

In their place Hemingway used a far more effective device. On the surface there was merely a fictional matador whose artistic ability and integrity suited Hemingway's purposes perfectly. Beneath the surface lay a historical reality which is never mentioned or alluded to in the published text of *The Sun Also Rises.* Submerged beneath the fictional character lay the real Pedro Romero.

Son and grandson of toreros, the serious, dignified matador from Ronda was unquestionably the greatest taurine artist of those waning years of the eighteenth century in which the Romero dynasty became the virtual founders of the modern art of toreo. Goya painted an exquisite portrait of him in his prime which reflects Romero's genius with no exaggeration or flourishes. To examine Goya's portrait of him—the assured grace, the understated elegance, the paradoxical delicacy of the prominently displayed right hand that dispatched 5,600 bulls in his long and unmarred career—is to encounter in Romero the prototype of the matador as the Spanish Romantic artist and popular hero. John Fulton, who is the only American to have written knowledgeably about the bulls from the unique vantage of a professional life as a matador, appraises Romero succinctly as "the most impressive matador in bullfighting history." The name Hemingway chose for his young matador as the measuring stick for the modern misfits of the

Lost Generation was perfect. And Hemingway's device was as brilliant as it was unobtrusive. The average reader would not be beleaguered by intrusive technical details, yet the aficionado would immediately perceive Hemingway's full meaning.

One final details assures us that Hemingway was consciously inventing from experience to create a superbly crafted work of art. In the rough draft, "Guerrita" kills the last bull in the usual manner, *volapié,* that is going to the bull. Yet in the finished version, with the descriptions of the corrida much augumented and revised, Romero kills in the far more difficult and dangerous manner called recibiendo or receiving the bull. The early version probably corresponds to the way "Niño de la Palma" actually fought and killed in Pamplona in 1925.

Why, then, did Hemingway revise it? In *Death in the Afternoon* he tells us that "Niño de la Palma" killed recibiendo "once in Madrid." And on July 16, 1925, Hemingway saw one of Cayetano Ordóñez's greatest afternoons in the Madrid plaza. He did not see him in Madrid again before the rewriting, so it is probable that the revisions in the corrida scene do not reflect what happened "as it was" merely in Pamplona but rather comprise an invention from experience based on a conflation or a distillation of the artistic success of Cayetano Ordóñez that Hemingway saw in Pamplona, Madrid, and Valencia that year.

But, Cayetano notwithstanding, there is a more compelling reason to explain the change. The historical Pedro Romero, as Hemingway knew, killed all the 5,600 bulls of his career recibiendo. It was only fitting, then, that the historical figure's newly created fictional avatar kill in the same manner. The aesthetic purity, the inherent danger, and the historical reverberation of Romero's kill recibiendo fittingly and elegantly enhance the climactic moment of the fiesta and of the novel. The changes, in effect, become important elements in the "making of the novel," and the metamorphosis of Cayetano Ordóñez into Pedro Romero becomes a splendid analogue for the transformation of certain events of the summer of 1925 into *The Sun Also Rises.* All that is left of Cayetano Ordóñez are a few brilliant moments of the season of 1925, moments that had originally inspired Hemingway to begin the novel. It is hardly accidental that he began with Cayetano but no less fortuitous that he ended with Pedro Romero, a fictional matador who, *mutatis mutandis,* owed much more to his legendary eighteenth-century namesake than to the benighted and already dissolute young man who, with no ruining from a Brett or a Duff, disappointed all Spain the following year.

The ficitonalizing of Pedro Romero, once we have seen Hemingway's revisions, allows us to return to a mythic consideration of toreo as the moral or spiritual axis of the novel. In the process of fictionalizing him, Hemingway made Romero into an idealized or moralized figure. We are not only dealing with a *paysage moralisé,* but with a *figure moralisée,* a kind of exemplar whose perfect sacrifice of the bull is the precise center and climactic moment of *The Sun Also Rises.* In fictionalizing his matador, Hemingway purified him (by contrast, all the other matadors mentioned in *The Sun Also Rises* are historical, real toreros), which is not to say that Romero is perfect—only that he is more worthy of being the sacrificer, more worthy that is of projecting us into sacred time. As Eliade put it:

> A sacrifice . . . not only exactly reproduces the initial sacrifice revealed by a god *ab origine,* at the beginning of time, it also takes place at that same primordial mythical moment; in other words, every sacrifice repeats the initial sacrifice and coincides with it. All sacrifices are performed at the same mythical instant of the beginning: through the paradox of rite, profane time and duration are suspended. And the same holds true for all repetitions, i.e., all limitations of archetypes; through such imitation, man is projected into the mythical epoch in which the archetypes were first revealed . . . insofar as an act . . . acquires a certain reality through the repetition of certain paradigmatic gestures, and acquires it through that alone, there is an implicit abolition of profane time, or duration, of "history"; and he who reproduces the exemplary gesture thus finds himself transported into the mythical epoch in which its revelation took place.

Hemingway, of course, had not read Eliade, but his subtle renaming of the matador and his intentional change to the exemplary kill recibiendo have quite the effect Eliade describes and transport us at once to that mythical epoch, to that first Golden Age, of the original Pedro Romero when modern toreo, the archetypal and paradigmatic art of toreo, was first created. Beyond that, toreo, at its deepest level, goes back much further and recapitulates as spectacle and as rite the oldest myths of the Western world. It is the art that structurally comes closer to the origin of art—the bull must still actually die—than any we know. Hemingway clearly understood, albeit somewhat intuitively, that toreo was at the still center of sacred time, and that it was *still* at the center of sacred time, still a part of the eternal present. His revisions provide rather irrefutable proof of his understanding and of his intentions.

Octavio Paz has written very lucidly about this eternal present in his penetrating essay, *The Labyrinth of Solitide.* "The fiesta," he tells us, "becomes the creator of time; repetition becomes conception. The golden age returns. . . . As Van der Leeuw said, 'all rituals have the property of taking place in the now, at this very instant.'" According to Paz, rituals and fiestas allow us to participate in mythical time:

> Thanks to participation, this mythical time— father of all the times that mask reality—coincides with our inner, subjective time. Man, the prisoner of succession, breaks out of his invisible jail and enters living time: his subjective life becomes identical with exterior time, because this has ceased to be a spatial measurement and has changed into a source, a spring, in the absolute present, endlessly re-creating itself. Myths and fiestas, whether secular or religious, permit man to emerge from his solitude and become one with creation.

Paz concludes his essay by reminding us that contemporary man has rationalized these things but not destroyed them. "Modern man," he warns, returning to his central image of the labyrinth, "likes to pretend that his thinking is wide-awake. But this wide-awake thinking has led us into the mazes of a nightmare in which the torture chambers are endlessly repeated in the mirrors of reason." It may be pretty to think that reason is our way and our light, but Paz and Eliade, and Jung and company, and Ernest Hemingway do not believe it. Beneath the nightmarish maze of pure reason lies a deeper and subliminally profound labyrinth, the archetypal labyrinth of so many ancient myths, one which has on rare occasions an extraordinarily exact ritual recapitulation in the arcane and sacrifical art of toreo. I once equated that ancient archetype and the art of toreo—rare perfect toreo, the most exact living configuration of the labyrinth and the most radical entry into sacred time we have left in the Western world—this way:

> And in the unchanging utopia of my mind's eye, *in illo tempore* of memory, I can still see—as once I actually did—a lone man, a motionless matador, standing in the center of an

ecstatic *plaza* as a great white bull charges and charges again, and the man, the matador, winds him and winds him again in inconceivably slow and successively longer arcs around his waist, spinning a lair for their common minotaur, through the sunlight, through the shadow, as though possessed of some ageless thread of Ariadne.

(White Wall of Spain)

What but such an entry into sacred time could Hemingway have had in mind when he described "the faena that takes a man out of himself and makes him feel immortal while it is proceeding, that gives him an ecstasy, that is, while momentary, as profound as any religious ecstasy"? What when he placed such a faena at the very center of *The Sun Also Rises,* a faena that the crowd did not ever want to be finished, but which was finished in Romero's exemplary, perfect, and paradigmatic kill recibiendo? And why if not to point up the sacred nature of this mythical novel of manners did he change his title from *Fiesta* (with its secondary English connotations of festivity, as opposed to Octavio Paz's use of the word in its Spanish sense, that is, a religious celebration such as the one celebrated in honor of San Fermin at Pamplona) to *The Sun Also Rises?* Why if not to contrast the sacred and the profane did he use as opposing epigraphs Gertrude Stein's otherwise utterly banal dictum "you are all a lost generation," which in context becomes a virtual maxim of historical and profane time, and the poignant and poetic quote from *Ecclesiastes,* the poetic, cyclical, and repetitive nature of which denies the importance of the individual or the individual generation and affirms the essence of sacred time in which, as Octavio Paz wrote, man emerges from his solitude and becomes one with creation?

At the still sunlit center of the book is the art of toreo, Romero's great faena and kill recibiendo, and around that in concentric circles, every one at a greater remove from the Promethean fire at the center, revolve first Romero himself, the mystagogue; then Montoya and the true aficionados, the priests; after that at varying distances Jake and Brett and the foreign aficionados, the not altogether faithful converts who make the pilgrimage to Pamplona seeking momentary solace in the fiesta; then farther away in near darkness the uninitiated American Ambassador and his entourage; and finally, altogether blind to the rising sun at the heart of the novel, alone and uncomprehending, Cohn. It was, as Hemingway said, a damn tragedy, the tragedy of his generation inescapably imprisoned in history, irredeemably lost in profane time, with the earth abiding forever as the only possible hero. *The Sun Also Rises*—his first, finest, and most profound novel—is Hemingway's tragedy of modern man's fall from primordial grace. If we fail to heed his prophetic admonition to our radically secular age, we only incur the graceless risk of accompanying Cohn in outer darkness.

Chronology

1899	Ernest Hemingway is born July 21 in Oak Park, Illinois.
1917	Works as reporter on *Kansas City Star*.
1918	Service in Italy with the American Red Cross; wounded on July 8 near Fossalta di Piave; affair with nurse Agnes von Kurowsky.
1920	Reporter for *Toronto Star*.
1921	Marries Hadley Richardson; moves to Paris.
1922	Reports Greco-Turkish War for *Toronto Star*.
1923	*Three Stories and Ten Poems* published in Paris. Son John born.
1924	A collection of vignettes, *in our time,* published in Paris by three mountains press.
1925	Attends Fiesta de San Fermin in Pamplona with Harold Loeb, Pat Guthrie, Duff Twysden, and others. *In Our Time*, which adds fourteen short stories to the earlier vignettes, is published in New York by Horace Liveright. It is Hemingway's first American book.
1926	*Torrents of Spring* and *The Sun Also Rises* published by Scribner's.
1927	*Men without Women* published. Marries Pauline Pfeiffer.
1928	Moves to Key West. Son Patrick born.
1929	*A Farewell to Arms.*
1931	Son Gregory born.
1932	*Death in the Afternoon.*
1933	*Winner Take Nothing.*
1935	*Green Hills of Africa.*
1937	*To Have and Have Not* published. Returns to Spain as war correspondent on the loyalist side.
1938	Writes script for the film *The Spanish Earth. The Fifth Column and the First Forty-Nine Stories* published.

1940   Marries Martha Gellhorn. *For Whom the Bell Tolls* published. Buys house in Cuba where he lives throughout most of the forties and fifties.

1942   Edits *Men at War*.

1944   Takes part in allied liberation of Paris with partisan unit.

1946   Marries Mary Welsh.

1950   *Across the River and into the Trees*.

1952   *The Old Man and the Sea*.

1954   Receives Nobel Prize for literature for *The Old Man and the Sea*.

1960   Settles in Ketchum, Idaho.

1961   Commits suicide on July 2 in Ketchum.

1964   *A Moveable Feast* published posthumously.

1970   *Islands in the Stream*.

1986   *The Garden of Eden*.

Contributors

HAROLD BLOOM, Sterling Professor of the Humanities at Yale University, is the author of *The Anxiety of Influence, Poetry and Repression*, and many other volumes of literary criticism. His forthcoming study, *Freud: Transference and Authority*, attempts a full-scale reading of all of Freud's major writings. A MacArthur Prize Fellow, he is the general editor of five series of literary criticism published by Chelsea House. During 1987–88, he was appointed Charles Eliot Norton Professor of Poetry at Harvard University.

CARLOS BAKER is Professor Emeritus of Literature at Princeton University, where he held the Woodrow Wilson Chair. Baker wrote the first full-length critical study of Hemingway's work, *Hemingway: The Writer as Artist*, in 1952. He is also the author of the definitive biography, *Ernest Hemingway: A Life Story*, and the editor of *Ernest Hemingway: Selected Letters, 1917–1961*.

MARK SPILKA is Professor of English at Brown University and the author of *The Love Ethic of D. H. Lawrence, Dickens and Kafka*, and *Virginia Woolf's Quarrel with Grieving*. He is currently at work on a book about Hemingway's Victorian literary models.

WILLIAM L. VANCE is Professor of English at Boston University.

ROBERT O. STEPHENS teaches at the University of North Carolina at Greensboro. He has published articles on colonial American literature and on Hemingway and F. Scott Fitzgerald.

JOSEPHINE Z. KNOPF is Professor of Humanities at Harcum Junior College and Adjunct Professor of Religion at Temple University. She specializes in writing about Jewish literature and religion.

SCOTT DONALDSON is a former faculty member of the College of William and Mary. He is the author of *The Life and Art of Ernest*

Hemingway and of books on Winfield Townley Scott and F. Scott Fitzgerald. His most recent work is *Conversations with John Cheever*.

CAROLE GOTTLIEB VOPAT is Professor of English at the University of Wisconsin-Parkside. Her doctoral dissertation was entitled "The Armored Self: A Study of Comparison and Control in *The Great Gatsby* and *The Sun Also Rises*."

LINDA W. WAGNER is Professor of English at Michigan State University and consulting editor for UMI Research Press. She is the author of *Hemingway and Faulkner: Inventors/ Masters*, as well as *Ernest Hemingway: A Reference Guide*, and the editor of an important anthology, *Ernest Hemingway: Five Decades of Criticism*.

MICHAEL S. REYNOLDS is Professor of English at North Carolina State University. He is the author of *Hemingway's First War: The Making of A Farewell to Arms*, *Hemingway's Reading, 1910–1940*, and the recent acclaimed biography, *The Young Hemingway*.

JAMES HINKLE is Professor of English at San Diego State University and editor of *The Faulkner Journal*. Hinkle has delivered numerous papers on Hemingway's work at national and international conferences in recent years. He is best-known for his work on *The Sun Also Rises* and has published several scholarly articles on the novel in *The Hemingway Review*.

ALLEN JOSEPHS is Professor of Spanish at the University of West Florida and the author of *White Wall of Spain: The Mysteries of Andalusian Culture*. He has edited *Federico Garcia Lorca: Antologia poetica* and, with Juan Caballero, two volumes of Garcia Lorca's poetry. Josephs is himself a published poet and is well-known in Hemingway circles for his scholarly articles on *Death in the Afternoon* and *The Sun Also Rises*.

Bibliography

Adams, Richard P. "Sunrise Out of *The Waste Land.*" *Tulane Studies in English* 9 (1959): 119–31.

Baker, Carlos. *Ernest Hemingway: A Life Story.* New York: Scribner's, 1969.

———, ed. *Ernest Hemingway: Selected Letters, 1917–1961.* New York: Scribner's, 1981.

———, ed. *Hemingway and His Critics: An International Anthology.* New York: Hill & Wang, 1961.

———, ed. *Hemingway: Critiques of Four Major Novels.* New York: Scribner's, 1962.

Baskett, Sam S. " 'An Image to Dance Around': Brett and Her Lovers in *The Sun Also Rises.*" *The Centennial Review* 22 (1978): 45–69.

Beach, Joseph Warren. *American Fiction: 1920–1940.* New York: Macmillan, 1941.

Benson, Jackson J. *Hemingway: The Writer's Art of Self-Defense.* Minneapolis: University of Minnesota Press, 1969.

Bloom, Harold, ed. *Modern Critical Views: Ernest Hemingway.* New York: Chelsea House, 1985.

Brenner, Gerry. "Hemingway's 'Vulgar' Ethic: *The Sun Also Rises.*" *Arizona Quarterly* 33 (1977): 101–15.

Bruccoli, Matthew J. *Scott and Ernest: The Authority of Failure and the Authority of Success.* New York: Random House, 1978.

Callaghan, Morley. *That Summer in Paris: Memories of Tangled Friendships with Hemingway, Fitzgerald, and Some Others.* New York: Coward-McCann, 1963.

Canby, Henry Seidel. *American Memoir.* Boston: Houghton Mifflin, 1947.

Capellan, Angel. *Hemingway and the Hispanic World.* Ann Arbor: University of Michigan Research Press, 1985.

Cochran, Robert W. "Circularity in *The Sun Also Rises.*" *Modern Fiction Studies* 14 (Autumn 1968): 255–70.

Cowan, S. A. "Robert Cohn, the Fool of Ecclesiastes in *The Sun Also Rises.*" *Dalhousie Review* 63, no. 1 (1983): 98–106.

Daiker, Donald A. "The Affirmative Conclusion of *The Sun Also Rises.*" *McNeese Review* 21 (1974–75): 3–19.

Donaldson, Scott. *By Force of Will: The Life and Art of Ernest Hemingway.* New York: Viking, 1977.

Gadjusek, Robert E., comp. *Hemingway's Paris.* New York: Scribner's, 1978.

Ganzel, Dewey. *"Cabestro* and *Vaquilla:* The Symbolic Structure of *The Sun Also Rises." The Sewanee Review* 76 (1968): 26–48.

Gordon, Gerald T. "Hemingway's Wilson-Harris: The Search for Value in *The Sun Also Rises."* In the *Fitzgerald/Hemingway Annual 1972,* edited by Matthew J. Bruccoli and C. E. Frazer Clark, Jr., 237–44. Columbia, S.C.: Bruccoli Clark, 1972.

———. "Survival in *The Sun Also Rises." Lost Generation Journal* 4, no. 2 (1976–77): 10–11, 17.

Grant, Mary Kathryn. "The Search for Celebration in *The Sun Also Rises* and *The Great Gatsby." Arizona Quarterly* 33 (1977): 181–92.

Grenberg, Bruce L. "The Design of Heroism in *The Sun Also Rises."* In the *Fitzgerald/Hemingway Annual 1971,* edited by Matthew J. Bruccoli and C.E. Frazer Clark, Jr., 274–89. Columbia, S.C.: Bruccoli Clark, 1971.

Griffin, Peter. *Along with Youth: Hemingway, the Early Years.* Oxford: Oxford University Press, 1985.

Hanneman, Audre. *Ernest Hemingway: A Comprehensive Bibliography.* Princeton: Princeton University Press, 1967.

———. *Supplement to Ernest Hemingway: A Comprehensive Bibliography.* Princeton: Princeton University Press, 1975.

The Hemingway Review 6, no. 1 (1986). [Issue commemorates the sixtieth anniversary of the publication of *The Sun Also Rises.*]

Hinkle, James. "Some Unexpected Sources for *The Sun Also Rises." The Hemingway Review* 2, no. 1 (1982): 26–42.

Hoffman, Frederick J. *The Twenties: American Writing in the Postwar Decade.* New York: Viking, 1955.

Hoffman, Michael J. "From Cohn to Herzog." *Yale Review* 58 (1969): 321–41.

Hook, Andrew. "Art and Life in *The Sun Also Rises."* In *Ernest Hemingway: New Critical Essays,* edited by Robert A. Lee, 49–63. Totowa, N. J.: Barnes & Noble, 1983.

Hovey, Richard B. *"The Sun Also Rises:* Hemingway's Inner Debate." *Forum* 4, no. 10 (1966): 4–10.

Huddleston, Sisley. *Paris Salons, Cafés, Studios: Being Social, Artistic, and Literary Memories.* Philadelphia: Lippincott, 1928.

Kert, Bernice. *The Hemingway Women.* New York: Norton, 1983.

Lauter, Paul. "Plato's Stepchildren, Gatsby and Cohn." *Modern Fiction Studies* 9 (1963–64): 338–46.

Lewis, Robert W., Jr. *Hemingway on Love.* Austin: University of Texas Press, 1965.

Liptzin, Sol. *The Jew in American Literature.* New York: Bloch, 1966.

Loeb, Harold. *The Way It Was.* New York: Criterion Books, 1959.

Lowenkron, David Henry. "Jake Barnes: A Student of William James in *The Sun Also Rises." The Texas Quarterly* 19, no. 1 (1976): 147–56.

McAlmon, Robert. *Being Geniuses Together, 1920–1930.* Garden City, N.Y.: Doubleday, 1968.

McCaffery, John K. M., ed. *Ernest Hemingway: The Man and His Work.* Cleveland: World, 1950.

Meyers, Jeffrey. *Hemingway: A Biography.* New York: Harper & Row, 1985.

———, ed. *Hemingway: The Critical Heritage.* London: Routledge & Kegan Paul, 1982.

Meyerson, Robert E. "Why Robert Cohn? An Analysis of Hemingway's *The Sun Also Rises.*" *Liberal and Fine Arts Review* 2, no. 1 (1982): 57–68.

Mizener, Arthur. *Twelve Great American Novels.* New York: New American Library, 1967.

Moore, Geoffrey. "*The Sun Also Rises:* Notes Toward an Extreme Fiction." *Review of English Literature* 4, no. 4 (1963): 31–46.

Mosher, Harold F., Jr. "The Two Styles of Hemingway's *The Sun Also Rises.*" In the *Fitzgerald/Hemingway Annual 1971,* edited by Matthew J. Bruccoli and C. E. Frazer Clark, Jr., 262–73. Columbia, S.C.: Bruccoli Clark, 1971.

Munson, Gorham. "A Comedy of Exiles." *The Literary Review* 12 (1968): 41–75.

Murphy, George D. "Hemingway's *Waste Land:* The Controlling Water Symbolism of *The Sun Also Rises.*" *Hemingway Notes* 1 (1971): 20–26.

Nelson, Gerald B. *Ten Versions of America.* New York: Knopf, 1972.

Newman, Paul B. "Hemingway's Grail Quest." *University of Kansas City Review* 28 (June 1962): 295–303.

Nichols, Kathleen L. "The Morality of Asceticism in *The Sun Also Rises:* A Structuralist Reinterpretation." In the *Fitzgerald/Hemingway Annual 1978,* edited by Matthew J. Bruccoli and Richard Layman, 321–30. Columbia, S.C.: Bruccoli Clark, 1978.

Phillips, Stephen R. "Hemingway and the Bullfight: The Archetypes of Tragedy." *Arizona Quarterly* 29 (1973): 37–56.

Pinsker, Sanford. "The Schlemiel in Yiddish and American Literature." *The Chicago Jewish Forum* 25 (1966-67): 191–95.

Plimpton, George. "The Art of Fiction, 21: Ernest Hemingway." *Paris Review* 5 (1958): 61–89.

Reardon, John. "Hemingway's Esthetic and Ethical Sportsmen." *The University Review* 34 (October 1967): 13–23.

Reynolds, Michael S. *Hemingway's Reading 1910-1940: An Inventory.* Princeton: Princeton University Press, 1976.

———. *The Young Hemingway.* Oxford: Basil Blackwell, 1986.

Rogers, Katherine M. *The Troublesome Helpmate: A History of Misogyny in Literature.* Seattle: University of Washington Press, 1966.

Ross, Morton L. "Bill Gorton: The Preacher in *The Sun Also Rises.*" *Modern Fiction Studies* 18 (1972–73): 517–27.

Rouch, John. "Jake Barnes as Narrator." *Modern Fiction Studies* 11 (1965-66): 361–70.

Rovit, Earl. *Ernest Hemingway.* New York: Twayne, 1963.

Sarason, Bertram D., ed. *Hemingway and the Sun Set.* Washington, D.C.: Microcard Editions, 1972.

Schneider, Daniel J. "The Symbolism of *The Sun Also Rises.*" *Discourse* 10 (1967): 337–42.

Schonhorn, Manuel. "*The Sun Also Rises:* I. The Jacob Allusion II. Parody as Meaning." *Ball State University Forum* 16, no. 2 (1975): 49–55.

Schwartz, Nina. "Lovers' Discourse in *The Sun Also Rises:* A Cock and Bull Story." *Criticism* 26, no. 1 (1984): 49–69.

Scott, Arthur. "In Defense of Cohn." *College English* 18 (1957): 309–14.

Seltzer, Leon F. "The Opportunity of Impotence: Count Mippopopolous in *The Sun Also Rises.*" *Renascence* 31 (1978): 3–14.

Sprague, Claire. *"The Sun Also Rises:* Its 'Clear Financial Basis.' " *American Quarterly* 21, no. 2 (1969): 259–66.

Stallman, R. W. *The Houses that James Built and Other Literary Studies.* East Lansing: Michigan State University Press, 1961.

Stephens, Robert O. *Hemingway's Nonfiction: The Public Voice.* Chapel Hill: University of North Carolina Press, 1968.

Stetler, Charles, and Gerald Locklin. "Does Time Heal All Wounds? A Search for the Code Hero in *The Sun Also Rises." McNeese Review* 28 (1981–82): 92–100.

Stoneback, H. R. " 'For Bryan's Sake': The Tribute to the Great Commoner in Hemingway's *The Sun Also Rises." Christianity and Literature* 32, no. 2 (1983): 29–36.

Stuckey, W. J. *"The Sun Also Rises* on Its Own Ground." *The Journal of Narrative Technique* 6 (1976): 224–32.

Sugg, Richard P. "Hemingway, Money, and *The Sun Also Rises."* In the *Fitzgerald/ Hemingway Annual 1972,* edited by Matthew J. Bruccoli and C. E. Frazer Clark, Jr., 257–67. Columbia, S.C.: Bruccoli Clark, 1972.

Svoboda, Frederic Joseph. *Hemingway and* The Sun Also Rises: *The Crafting of a Style.* Lawrence: University Press of Kansas, 1983.

Torchiana, Donald T. *"The Sun Also Rises:* A Reconsideration." In the *Fitzgerald/ Hemingway Annual 1969,* edited by Matthew J. Bruccoli, 77–103. Columbia, S.C.: Bruccoli Clark, 1969.

Wagner, Linda W. *Ernest Hemingway: Five Decades of Criticism.* East Lansing: Michigan State University Press, 1974.

Waldhorn, Arthur. *A Reader's Guide to Ernest Hemingway.* New York: Farrar, Straus & Giroux, 1972.

Watkins, Floyd C. *The Flesh and the Word: Eliot, Hemingway, Faulkner.* Nashville: Vanderbilt University Press, 1971.

Wedin, Warren. "Trout Fishing and Self-Betrayal in *The Sun Also Rises." Arizona Quarterly* 37 (1981): 63–74.

Westbrook, Max, ed. *The Modern American Novel: Essays in Criticism.* New York: Random House, 1966.

White, William, ed. *The Merrill Studies in* The Sun Also Rises. Columbus, Ohio: Merrill, 1969.

Wylder, Delbert E. *Hemingway's Heroes.* Albuquerque: University of New Mexico Press, 1969.

———. "The Two Faces of Brett: The Role of the New Woman in *The Sun Also Rises." Kentucky Philological Association Bulletin* (1980): 27–33.

Yevish, Irving A. "The Sun Also Exposes: Hemingway and Jake Barnes." *Midwest Quarterly* 10 (1968): 89–97.

Young, Philip. *Ernest Hemingway: A Reconsideration.* University Park: Pennsylvania State University Press, 1966.

Young, Philip, and Charles W. Mann, comps. *The Hemingway Manuscripts: An Inventory.* University Park: Pennsylvania State University Press, 1969.

Zehr, David Morgan. "Paris and the Expatriate Mystique: Hemingway's *The Sun Also Rises." Arizona Quarterly* 33 (1977): 156–64.

Acknowledgments

"The Wastelanders" by Carlos Baker from *Hemingway: The Writer as Artist* by Carlos Baker, © 1956, 1963, 1972, 1980 by Carlos Baker. Chapter 4 reprinted by permission of Princeton University Press.

"The Death of Love in *The Sun Also Rises*" by Mark Spilka from *Twelve Original Essays on Great American Novels,* edited by Charles Shapiro, © 1958 by Wayne State University Press. Reprinted by permission.

"Implications of Form in *The Sun Also Rises*" by William L. Vance from *The Twenties, Poetry and Prose: Twenty Critical Essays,* edited by Richard E. Langford and William E. Taylor, © 1966 by Everett Edwards Press, Inc. Reprinted by permission.

"Ernest Hemingway and the Rhetoric of Escape" by Robert O. Stephens from *The Twenties, Poetry and Prose: Twenty Critical Essays,* edited by Richard E. Langford and William E. Taylor, © 1966 by Everett Edwards Press, Inc. Reprinted by permission.

"Meyer Wolfsheim and Robert Cohn: A Study of a Jewish Type and Stereotype" by Josephine Z. Knopf from *Tradition: A Journal of Orthodox Jewish Thought* 10, no. 3 (Spring 1969), © 1969 by the Rabbinical Council of America. Reprinted by permission. The notes have been omitted.

"Hemingway's Morality of Compensation" by Scott Donaldson from *American Literature* 43, no. 3 (November 1971), © 1971 by Duke University Press. Reprinted by permission.

"The End of *The Sun Also Rises:* A New Beginning" by Carole Gottlieb Vopat from *The Fitzgerald/Hemingway Annual, 1972,* edited by Matthew J. Bruccoli and C. E. Frazer Clark, Jr., © 1973 by the National Cash Register Company, Dayton, Ohio. Reprinted by permission.

"*The Sun Also Rises:* One Debt to Imagism" by Linda W. Wagner from *The Journal of Narrative Technique* 2, no. 2 (May 1972), © 1972 by Eastern Michigan University Press. Reprinted by permission.

"False Dawn: *The Sun Also Rises* Manuscript" by Michael S. Reynolds from *A Fair Day in the Affections: Literary Essays in Honor of Robert B. White, Jr.,* edited by

Jack D. Durant and M. Thomas Hester, © 1980 by Jack D. Durant and M. Thomas Hester. Reprinted by permission.

"What's Funny in *The Sun Also Rises*" by James Hinkle from *The Hemingway Review* 4, no. 2 (Spring 1985), © 1985 by Ohio Northern University. Reprinted by permission.

"*Toreo*: The Moral Axis of *The Sun Also Rises*" by Allen Josephs from *The Hemingway Review* 6, no. 1 (Fall 1986), © 1986 by Ohio Northern University. Reprinted by permission.

Index

Adams, Nick (*In Our Time*), 30, 31, 32, 34, 57, 153

Adventures of Augie March, The (Bellow), 46, 48

Adventures of Huckleberry Finn, The (Twain), 1, 6, 46–47

A la recherche du temps perdu (Proust), 69–70

Algren, Nelson, 5

American Procession, An (Kazin), 151

Anderson, Sherwood, 12

Arlen, Michael, 12, 120

Art of Ernest Hemingway, The (Atkins), 133

Ashley, Lady Brett, 5, 7, 131, 154; as allegorical figure, 25; ambivalent characterization of, 14, 22–23, 83–84, 106; and awareness of nada, 53–54; biographical prototype for, 11, 84, 121; as Circe, 19–20, 22; and distortion of sex roles, 28–29, 36; and double meanings, 137; egotism of, 47–48, 82–83; and episodic structure, 39, 41, 42, 44–46; and Frances Clyne, 107; and guilt, 94; and humor, 142, 143; hunger of, 99; illusions of, 99, 100–101; and immediacy as value, 53; and Jake Barnes, 40, 91–92, 98–99; language of, 54; maturation of, 97, 111; meanness of, 48; and Mike Campbell, 81; morality of, 17, 76, 77, 83–84; as neurotic, 14, 15; as Pallas Athene, 19; and religion, 21–22, 137–38; and romanticism, 27; and sexual humor, 147-48, 149; sexuality of, 83;

strength of, 29, 105; as victim of war, 23–24, 83; and violence as degradation, 35–36

Atkins, John, 133

Auerbach, Erich, 6

Auroras of Autumn, The (Stevens), 6

Austen, Jane, 28

Baker, Carlos, 77, 83–84, 125

Barkley, Catherine (*A Farewell to Arms*), 29

Barnes, Jake, 131, 154; as allegorical figure, 25; ambivalent characterization of, 106; and anti-Semitism, 67; and awareness of nada, 53; and Brett Ashley, 22–23, 40, 91–93, 98–100, 122, 136, 138; and bullfighting as sacred, 158; compassion of, 94, 96–97; compulsiveness of, 92–93; and control, 95, 100, 101; corruption of, 132; courage of, 95; disillusionment of, 97–98, 100; and distortion of sex roles, 36; as emotional adolescent, 34–35, 36; emotional duplicity of, 46; and episodic structure, 39, 43, 44; as Hamlet, 11; and homosexuals, 144; and humor, 133, 135–36, 139–40, 141–42, 147, 148–49; hunger of, 99–100; and imagistic style, 112–13; impotence of, 7, 26, 93–94, 148–49; and intimacy, 114; and irony, 55; and jealousy, 42; and language, 54–55, 56, 112; and love, 111; and male companionship, 15, 16–17;

Barnes, Jake *(continued)*
   masculinity of, 23, 101, 112;
   maturation of, 7–8, 58, 91–101;
   meanness of, 48; and money, 73,
   75–77; morality of, 15, 26, 30,
   75–76, 77, 98–99; and morality of
   compensation, 72–73, 88; as
   narrator, 40, 41, 46, 57, 58, 105–6;
   and ocean, 95–96; as Odysseus,
   19; and Pedro Romero, 32;
   pragmatism of, 52; and religion,
   20–21, 137–38; and Robert Cohn,
   33–34, 41–42; and romanticism,
   27, 28, 91, 92; as self-portrait of
   Hemingway, 14; silence of, 112;
   and solitude, 94–95; and sports,
   30–31; strength of, 14, 29, 105;
   and work, 75; wound of, 121–22,
   147–48
Bellow, Saul, 46, 48
Belmonte, 84, 85, 128
Bird, Wiliam, 103
Bishop, John Peale, 9, 103
Bloch (*A la recherche du temps perdu*),
   69–70
Braddocks, Mr., 12, 28, 146
Braddocks, Mrs., 12, 28, 53, 144, 146
Bradley, Helene (*Across the River and
   into the Trees*), 89
Bullfighting: as ancient mystery, 153;
   and commercialism, 84–85;
   Hemingway's discovery of,
   152–53; matador as messiah in,
   5, 157, 161, 162; as measure of
   morality, 154–55, 156–57; as
   sacred, 156, 157, 158–59, 164–67
Burke, Kenneth, 8

Campbell, Mike, 5; ambivalent
   characterization of, 106;
   biographical prototype for, 11,
   121; and Brett Ashley, 23, 138;
   and humor, 137, 142; and
   language, 56; and money,
   80–82; moral decadence of, 77;
   and myth, 19; as neurotic, 14,
   15; and Robert Cohn, 32
Cantwell, Col. Robert (*Across the
   River and into the Trees*), 57, 89
Carraway, Nick (*The Great Gatsby*),
   47, 65, 120

Cather, Willa, 47
Chekov, Anton, 47
Chrome Yellow (Huxley), 19
Clemens, Samuel. *See* Twain, Mark
Clyne, Frances, 27, 28, 42, 76, 80, 107,
   114
Cohn, Robert: as allegorical figure, 25;
   biographical prototype for, 11,
   79, 121, 133; and Brett Ashley, 23;
   characterization of, 107; as
   contrast to moral norm, 16, 17,
   18, 47, 77, 78–80, 107; and
   distortion of sex roles, 29; as
   Elpenor, 20; emptiness of, 18,
   33, 158, 166, 167; and episodic
   structure, 43–44; as false
   expatriate, 53; importance of,
   40–41, 46; and Jake Barnes, 33–
   34; as Jewish stereotype, 5, 62, 66,
   67–69, 70; lack of charm of, 69;
   language of, 144–45; and male
   companionship, 17; and money,
   73, 79–80; and myth, 19; as
   neurotic, 14, 15; vs. Pedro
   Romero, 18; regression to
   adolescence of, 34; as romantic,
   26–27, 32–33, 44, 91; as
   scapegoat, 32; and sequential
   structure, 41, 42–43, 44–45; as
   shlemiel, 67–69; as social
   commentator, 68; and violence,
   45; and women, 80
Complete Aficionado, The (McCormick),
   154–55
Conrad, Joseph, 6
Cook, R. L., 20
Corrochano, Gregorio, 161
Counter-Statement (Burke), 8
Cowley, Malcolm, 59–60, 74

Daisy (*The Great Gatsby*), 47–48
Death in the Afternoon, 58, 111,
   131–32; bullfighting as sacred
   in, 153, 155–56, 157; portrayal of
   Guerrita in, 129; portrayal of
   Niño de la Palma in, 126–27, 163
"Death of Love in *The Sun Also Rises*"
   (Spilka), 93
de la Palma, Niño, 11, 121, 126–27,
   128, 129, 160–61, 163
Dickinson, Emily, 71–72

Dos Passos, John, 88, 151
Dreiser, Theodore, 48
Duzinell, Madame, 83

"Echoes of the Jazz Age" (Fitzgerald), 62
Eliade, Mircea, 158–59, 164
Eliot, T. S., 19, 20, 22, 25, 106
Emerson, Ralph Waldo, 71
Exile's Return (Cowley), 59–60
Ezra, Ibn, 66

Farewell to Arms, A, 10, 29, 120; escape in, 51; language in, 56; manuscript of, 122; morality in, 72, 89; as personal exorcism, 11; plot of, 124, 125; pragmatism in, 52; repetition in, 110; rhetorical stance of, 6; understatement in, 4, 5
Farrell, James T., 72
Fischer, Doc ("God Rest You Merry, Gentlemen"), 3
Fitzgerald, F. Scott, 9, 99, 153; anti-Semitism of, 62, 70; influence on Hemingway of, 12, 13, 119. *See also Great Gatsby, The*
Fletcher, Angus, 6
Ford, Ford Madox, 122
From Shylock to Svengali: Jewish Stereotypes in English Fiction (Rosenberg), 64
Fulton, John, 162

Gamble, James, 152
"Gimpel the Fool" (Singer), 69
Girones, Vicente, 95
Gorton, Bill: and awareness of nada, 53; biographical prototype for, 12, 77; and Brett Ashley, 23; and humor, 133, 135, 143, 146; and irony, 55; and language, 56–57; likeableness of, 77–78; and male companionship, 15, 16–17; and Mike Campbell, 81; and money, 78; and morality, 15, 78; and music, 145; and Robert Cohn, 78, 80; solidity of, 14; and sports, 30–31

Great American Novel, The (Williams), 104
Great Gatsby, The (Fitzgerald), 120; Jewish stereotype in, 61, 62, 63–66, 69, 70; romantic vs. episodic in, 47, 48
Green Hat, The (Arlen), 12
Guerra, Rafael, 129, 130, 156
Guerrita. *See* Guerra, Rafael
Gutherie, Pat, 121

Harcourt, Alfred, 9
Hassan, Ihab, 113–14
Hawthorne, Nathaniel, 47
Hemingway, Ernest: ambition of, 3; anti-Semitism of, 62, 70; on bullfighting, 152–53, 159; on characters, 71; and Conrad, 6; divorce of, 121; and Emersonian tradition, 3; on expatriates, 74–75; and Fitzgerald, 119–20; on humor, 134; influences on, 1–3; and James, 125; life of, 5; and "lost generation," 10–11, 13–14, 119; love of nature of, 14; on morality, 72; as poet, 2–3, 104; and Pound, 103–4, 106; rhetorical stance of, 6; as short-story writer, 3–5; and Spain, 152–53; and Stevens, 2; on *The sun Also Rises,* 14; and Turgenev, 123; and Twain, 1; on wealth, 88–89; and Whitman, 1–2; on work, 75; as writer of despair, 58; as writer-wanderer, 151–52; writing methods of, 9–10, 122. Works: *Across the River and into the Trees,* 57, 89; "Along with Youth," 104; "Big Two-Hearted River," 30, 31–32, 124, 153; *The Dangerous Summer,* 153, 160; *The First Forty-Nine Stories,* 2; *For Whom the Bell Tolls,* 4, 20, 89; "God Rest You Merry Gentlemen," 3; *Green Hills of Africa,* 88; *In Our Time,* 34, 51, 57, 58–59, 104–5; "Indian Camp," 124; *Men Without Women,* 10, 51; *A Moveable Feast,* 75, 79, 88, 118, 122; "A Natural History of the Dead," 3; "Oklahoma," 104; *The*

Hemingway, Ernest (continued)
Old Man and the Sea, 35, 89;
"Old Man at the Bridge," 4; "On
Writing," 153; "The Short
Happy Life of Francis Macomber,"
35, 89; The Snows of
Kilimanjaro, 88–89, 138–39; "Ten
Indians," 132; Three Stories and
Ten Poems, 104; To Have and Have
Not, 4, 89; The Torrents of
Spring, 10, 120, 134; Winner Take
Nothing, 6, 51
Hemingway, Hadley, 121
Hemingway's fiction: episodic struc-
ture in, 58–60; escape in, 51–52,
57–58; imagist influence on,
103–5; indirect focus in, 131;
isolation in, 113–14; morality of
compensation in, 72, 89; myth
in, 19–20; paragraphs in, 58–59;
parataxis in, 6–7; as personal
exorcism, 10–11; pragmatism in,
52; psychological symbolism in,
20; repetition in, 59, 110; sports
in, 30; understatement in, 4–5,
7; war vs. love in, 23–24
Hemingway's First War (Reynolds), 122
Henry, Fredric (A Farewell to Arms),
52, 56, 57, 89
Hobin, Georgette, 28, 29, 55, 73,
75–76, 146
Hoffman, F. J., 59
Hollander, John, 6
Horne, William D., 152
Hovey, Richard, 91
Huxley, Aldous, 19
Hyman, Stanley Edgar, 111

Indiscretions (Pound), 104

James, Henry, 125, 126
Jenkins, Howell, 152
Jordan, Robert (For Whom the Bell
Tolls), 57, 89
Joyce, James, 19, 20

Kafka, Franz, 34
Kazin, Alfred, 151, 158
Keats, John, 20

Krum, 112

Labyrinth of Solitude, The (Paz), 165
Lawrence, D. H., 25
Levin, Harry, 54
Lewis, Sinclair, 12
Littell, Robert, 11, 12
Loeb, Harold, 79, 121, 133

McCormick, John, 154–55, 156, 158
Macomber, Margot ("The Short
Happy Life of Francis
Macomber"), 89
McTeague (Norris), 48
Marlow (Heart of Darkness; Lord Jim), 6
Matador, as messiah. See Bullfighting
Meeber, Carrie, 106
Mippipopolous, Count, 83, 124, 143;
and awareness of nada, 53;
biographical prototype for, 12;
controlled life of, 96; and
humor, 147; and immediacy of
value, 53; and language, 54,
133; and money, 73; and morality
of compensation, 87–88
Miss Lonelyhearts (West), 3
Montoya, 35, 85, 121, 125, 137,
158
Morality: bullfighting as measure of,
154–55, 156–57; and compensa-
tion, 72–73, 78, 87–90; contrasts
in, 15–19, 22, 24, 77;
Hemingway on, 72; and money,
77, 79–80, 88; and work, 75
Morgan, Harry (To Have and Have
Not), 89
Murphy, Sara, 2
My Antonia (Cather), 47
Myth of the Eternal Return, The
(Eliade), 158–59

Ney, Marshal, 148
Nietzsche, Friedrich, 8
Norris, Frank, 48

O'Brien, Edward J., 152
O'Connor, Frank, 139
O'Hara, John, 5

Ortóñez, Cayetano. *See* de la Palma, Niño

Paz, Octavio, 165, 166
Perkins, Maxwell, 14, 18, 119, 121, 145, 159
Pilar (*For Whom the Bell Tolls*), 20
Plimpton, George, 7
Portrait of the Artist as a Young Man, A (Joyce), 19
Pound, Ezra, 103–4, 106, 107, 109, 110, 112, 115, 153
Prentiss, Robert, 12, 28, 52, 144
Proust, Marcel, 70

Quintana. *See* Montoya

Rindalda (*A Farewell to Arms*), 124
Romero, Pedro, 5, 45, 83; as allegorical figure, 25; biographical prototypes for, 11, 121, 126–28, 129–30, 156, 162–63; betrayal of, 7; and Brett Ashley, 23; and commercialism, 84, 85; disillusionment of, 97; and double meanings, 137; fictionalizing of, 159–64; greatness of, 37, 95, 96, 99, 156–57; as ideal, 18, 22, 58, 126, 127–28, 129, 158, 164; masculinity of, 33, 35–36, 91; morality of, 14, 15; and morality of compensation, 85, 89; vs. Robert Cohn, 18; style of, 92; and violence as degradation, 35–36
Rosenberg, Edgar, 64
Ross, Lillian, 110
Rouch, John, 91

Santiago (*The Old Man and the Sea*), 89
Sanz, Cayetano, 161
Scarlet Letter, The (Hawthorne), 47
Schorer, Mark, 115
Scribner, Charles, 3
"Serious Artist, The" (Pound), 110
Shakespeare, William, 20
Shrike (*Miss Lonelyhearts*), 3
Singer, Isaac Bashevis, 69
Sister Carrie (Dreiser), 48

Spilka, Mark, 91, 93
Sportsman's Sketches, A (Turgenev), 122–23
Stein, Gertrude, 13, 19, 59, 105, 118–19, 166
Stevens, Wallace, 2, 6
Stewart, Donald Ogden, 77, 133
Stone, Harvey, 34, 53
Stoneback, H. R., 155
Sun Also Rises, The: as allegory, 25; allusion in, 56–57; anti-Semitism in, 62, 146; awareness of nada in, 53–54, 55; biographical prototypes for characters in, 11–12, 121; bullfighting as heart of, 153–67; character development in, 106–7, 126; Christianity vs. paganism in, 20–22; circular structure in, 39, 58, 93; commercialism in, 84–86; conclusion of, 125; criticism of, 11; death in, 128; death of love in, 25–37; dedication of, 120–21; deliberate misunderstanding in, 141–42; disillusionment in, 97, 99, 100; distortion of sex roles in, 28–29, 36–37; double meanings in, 136–38; epigraphs of, 13, 17, 37, 39, 58, 105, 119, 166; escape in, 52–60; first-person narration in, 105–6; foreign stereotypes in, 86–87; geography of, 155; hell as image in, 140–41; Hemingway's distance from, 10–11, 14; historical setting of, 74, 117; homosexuals in, 144; humor in, 133–49; image of ocean in, 95–96; immediacy as value in, 53; impotence in, 26, 29; indirect focus in, 130–31; influence of imagism on, 105–15; irony in, 55; juxtaposition in, 108; lack of symbols in, 110–11; language in, 54–57, 59; limitations of, 5; literal humor in, 138, 139–41; "lost generation" in, 10–11, 12–13, 14, 17, 105, 118–19; male companionship in, 15–16; manuscript versions of, 117–32, 159–62, 163; misreading of, 105; monetary transactions in, 73–74; mortality of compensation in, 72–90; moral

Sun Also Rises, The (continued)
counterpoint in, 15–19, 22, 24, 72, 77; myth in, 19–20; narrative voice in, 40, 41, 46; nature in, 15–17; opening of, 124–25; parataxis in, 7; Pedro Romero as center of, 126–30; prose rhythms in, 108–10; religion in, 31, 137–38, 155; repetition in, 59; rhetorical stance in, 6; role of shlemiel in, 67–68; romanticism in, 26–28; sadness of, 114, 132; sequential structure in, 41; as series of vignettes, 4; sexual humor in, 147–49; as social history, 13; "special moment" in, 125–26; sports in, 30–31, 37; strengths of, 5–6, 8; structure of, 39–49, 123–25; as study of love, 111, 114; success of, 12; three-book division of, 121; title of, 117–19, 166; tourists in, 85; use of detail in, 106; varying interpretations of, 154; violence as degradation in, 34–35; war vs. love in, 23–24; working titles of, 117–19; writing process of, 9–10
Swann (*A la recherche du temps perdu*), 70

This Side of Paradise (Fitzgerald), 12, 13
Thoreau, Henry David, 20

Three Sisters (Chekov), 47
Toreo. *See* Bullfighting
"Tragic, The" (Emerson), 71
Turgenev, Ivan Sergeyevich, 122–23
Twain, Mark, 1, 6, 46–47
Twenties, The (Hoffman), 59
Twysden, Duff, 84, 121

Ulysses (Joyce), 19, 20

Van der Leeuw, 165

Warren, Robert Penn, 2, 4, 52
Waste Land, The (Eliot), 19, 20, 25
Watkins, Floyd, 111
West, Nathanael, 3
Wharton, Edith, 63
White Wall of Spain (Josephis), 165–66
Whitman, Walt, 1–2
Williams, William Carlos, 104, 113
Wilson-Harris, 12, 31, 55, 56, 86, 112
Winesburg, Ohio (Anderson), 12
Wolfsheim, Meyer (*The Great Gatsby*), 61, 62, 63–66, 69, 70
Woolsey, 112

Young, Philip, 72, 89, 91, 122

Zizi, 53